The magic … had No. 1
hits in ever… America;
in Britain t… atinum and
silver discs … ales topped
40 million i… Beatles; and
their charm and Swedish good looks have captured hearts whereever they have appeared.

At the centre of this whirlwind of success are four young people with doubts and fears, loves and hates, problems and passions. Anni-Frid was the despised daughter of a Norwegian girl and a German soldier; Benny's past is clouded by a secret girlfriend who cares for his two children; Bjorn is a frustrated intellectual, a dropped-out undergraduate who has to remember to smile on stage, involved in a running battle with critics who say his music is plastic; Agnetha is a country girl who hid her shyness beneath a mask of arrogance.

And there is a fifth member of Abba: the shadowy Stikkan Andersson, an ex-schoolteacher who turned Swedish show-business upside-down with his controversial methods and his relentless hunger for success.

Their problems, their secrets, their love for each other: here for the first time is the whole story behind the new Beatles – the truth about Abba.

# THE AUTHORS

Harry Edgington, 35, is a former *Daily Sketch* reporter who has served as Hollywood correspondent for the *Daily Mail*, the *Daily Mirror*, and *The Sun*. Now a freelance journalist and author, he has co-authored *Shake A Pagoda Tree* – the autobiography of Mike and Bernie Winters – *How To Survive in the Nick, The Story of the Goons* and *Bomb Squad*. He splits his working life between London, Los Angeles, and various parts of Europe.

Peter Himmelstrand, 40, spans triple careers as a journalist, lyric writer, composer, and record producer. He was music columnist of *Expressen*, Sweden's leading evening newspaper, for fifteen years. Among the artistes he has penned hit records for are three members of Abba, Bjorn Ulvaeus, Benny Andersson, and Agnetha Faltskog. He has been a close confidant of the Abba team and of their 'fifth member', Stikkan Andersson, since their earliest days in showbusiness. Peter lives in Huddinge, Sweden, with his girlfriend, Annika, and two children from a previous marriage.

# ABBA

Harry Edgington
and
Peter Himmelstrand

MAGNUM BOOKS
Methuen Paperbacks Ltd

**A Magnum Book**

ABBA

ISBN 0 417 03370 2

First published in Great Britain 1977
by Everest Books Ltd
Magnum revised edition published 1978


Cover photograph: Sport and General Press Agency

Magnum Books are published
by Methuen Paperbacks Ltd
11 New Fetter Lane, London EC4P 4EE

Made and printed in Great Britain
by Hazell Watson & Viney Ltd
Aylesbury, Bucks

## CONTENTS

CHAPTER ONE

# ANNI-FRID

The more polite friends of the young Norwegian girl ignored her when they passed in the street. The others either swore at her or spat on the pavement. Her crime? She had fallen in love with a German officer, one of the army which had kept Norway under its heel during the wartime years, and was expecting his child.

It was 1945, just after the end of the war, and this was Narvik, a town in the far north of Norway which had seen the ignominious flight of the British and French soldiers in 1940 and since then gone through all the pain of being a defensive outpost of the Third Reich. The German occupiers – and their brutal methods – were hated and feared by the local population. For four years, they had no choice but to bend the knee to the invaders. But when Synni Lyngstad, an innocent nineteen-year-old, came face to face with that officer, Alfred Haase, he seemed somehow different to the others. To her, he was a young man forced to leave his loved ones to take up a duty he abhorred. She listened to him talking about the home and parents he missed, his friends. He was different to the other jackbooted officers strutting around town. They started meeting in what they thought were clandestine encounters. In fact, everybody in town knew about them and talked about Synni and her German lover. Her relatives tried to warn her. 'You must keep away from him,' they said. 'He may be kind and gentle, but he is a German. The war will be over soon, but no-one here will forget this business.' Sadly, they were right. At the end of the war, the young Alfred was shipped back to Germany. Before he left, he promised to return to marry his Synni. But he never came back.

Their child, a daughter, was born on 15 November 1945, and named Anni-Frid after Synni's grandmother. That winter was the coldest Europe had known for years, but the ice was warmer than the feelings the people of Narvik had for Synni – and her daughter. They still hated in Norway, and the locals spat out the name given by Norwegians to all the babies born to Norwegian girls from the German soldier fathers – 'tysk-barn', which means 'German child'.

For nearly two years, Synni Lyngstad waited in Narvik for her wartime lover to return. Her mother watched her slowly pining away amidst her unhappiness and loneliness and the hate heaped on her. Synni died when she was just twenty-one. The grandmother realised that little Anni-Frid, with the tag 'German child', would have a miserable time if she stayed to grow up in Narvik. So she gathered a few possessions and took the girl to Sweden, where no-one would know of her beginnings and where she could live a normal life. They moved from one small country town to another, the grandmother earning enough to keep them by working as a seamstress. For years they were on the move, until finally they settled in the village of Torshälla. This is where Anni-Frid grew up.

When Anni-Frid talks about these days, a misty look comes over her face and you can see her feeling the suffering her mother went through. 'I feel so sad for her,' she says. 'To think of a young girl having all that unhappiness. But I do not blame my father. I don't think it was his fault. I think he was as much a victim of the war as she was. I would like to have met him. I am sure he wanted to come back to Norway to marry her but that something happened to prevent him doing it. I have tried to find him but that is obviously very difficult. I don't think he ever got back to Germany. From what I have been able to find out, I believe his troopship was sunk off Denmark in one of the last actions of the war. So while my mother was waiting for him to return, his body was probably at the bottom of the sea.

'I have been back to Narvik since, to visit my relatives. People don't hate there any more and it is hard to imagine how they looked to my mother. But to them, for her to love a German was absolutely inexcusable. After all these years, we perhaps find it difficult to believe that essentially kind people could carry so much resentment, but then we do not know what it is like to be occupied by a foreign army.'

The young Anni-Frid was brought up as a Swedish citizen, and she now considers herself very much Swedish, rather than Norwegian. Because she could never remember her real mother, she has always called her grandmother 'Mama', and still does.

Anni-Frid has fond memories of those childhood days with her grandmother. 'She was always so kind to me, and encouraged me in anything I did,' she recalls. 'I particularly remember the long, dark, and cold winter evenings when we would sit together round the fire and she would teach me to sing old Swedish and Norwegian folk songs. It was Mama who encouraged me to sing, and it was she who helped me to discover that I could sing, and enjoyed singing.'

At the age of ten, Anni-Frid sang her first engagement. On stage at the local village hall, entertaining the other children – and a few of the adults, too. She did not have a trace of stage nerves. However, later she was to find that her nervousness was to grow in proportion to the engagement and its importance.

She moved fluently on to her debut as a dance band singer in a restaurant club at Eskilstuna, a town near Stockholm that she and her grandmother moved to. Anni-Frid was just thirteen years old, officially too young to appear in such an establishment. She overcame this small problem by lying about her age, adding three years on. She got away with it because she looked mature enough and, perhaps more important, her singing matched this impression. It was the true beginning of her apprenticeship.

Within a couple of years, she had her own dance band – The Anni-Frid Four – which backed her singing in the local nightspots around Eskilstuna, three or four nights a week.

'They were really fun days,' she remembers. 'We were getting paid, but I was singing for fun, because I really enjoyed it. And the band were always so relaxed and happy. They had that carefree air of bands, which you only find in small supper clubs. There was no great pressure on them, and their playing – and their smiling faces – betrayed the contentment they felt.'

The bass player and leader of the band was a furniture salesman, Ragnar Fredriksson. Anni-Frid liked the way he handled the musicians. She also liked him. They started to date, and fell in love. They got engaged and, in the Swedish fashion, started living together. At the age of sixteen, she had a son, Hans. The year after they married and later had another child, a daughter, Lise-Lotte. She also kept up her musical partnership with Ragnar, and they toured together, leaving the children in the care of her grandmother.

When she was eighteen she entered an amateur singing contest in the nearby town of Vasteras. The tall, beautiful girl with a red dress matching her reddish-brown hair, knocked the judges out with her powerful rendering of the Spanish song 'Besame Mucho'. Called up to collect her prize, she shyly told how she had learned the melody on her honeymoon in the Canary Islands. The lyrics she learned from a record, and a Spanish-speaking friend translated the words for her. Leading the applause in the audience was Ragnar, who was so happy for her. He had no way of knowing that this victory was the first of a chain of events which were inevitably to take Anni-Frid away from him. For Anni-Frid was, and still is, a girl with big ambitions. The band, she knew, was adequate for her appearances in the restaurants, but she also knew that if she was to make her way in showbusiness – as she was sure she could – she would have to work with better musicians. The better musicians were in Stockholm, and it was to Stockholm she went in 1967 to take part in an all-Sweden 'New Faces' talent contest organised by the childrens' charity, Barnens Dag. She won, singing a ballad called 'A Day Off'.

Afterwards the compere asked her: 'What are you going to do now?'

A very happy Anni-Frid answered: 'I'm going home to sleep.'

'Oh, no, you are not,' said the compere. 'Outside this door is a car which is going to take you to appear on a television show.'

The astonished and bewildered Anni-Frid was whisked into a television chat show, where she was asked what job she did. Her answer was: 'I am married and have two children. That is my profession.' That was not to be true for very much longer.

She got on to a television show and suddenly everybody wanted the honey-voiced Anni-Frid to sing for them. She went on tours round the *folkparks*, the summer entertainment centres which were set up at the turn of the century when the Swedish government decided that every town and village should have its own outdoor amusements. This time Anni-Frid recalls as 'a long-term exercise in keeping on the move and keeping fit – but it was also a lot of fun'. She said: 'Despite the rigours of the hectic travelling – because the *folkparks* are spread far and wide all over the country – and the poor facilities the artistes had to put up with at some of the smaller centres, I always enjoyed those tours. I suppose you can compare the *folkparks* circuit to the old music halls in England and vaudeville in the United States, where performers learned their business. It's a hard school, but a good one. And, of course, Sweden is a lovely country to travel in, especially in the summer. So my memory tells me those were some of the best days of my life. But I do wonder if it is a case of my memory being kind to history. What they certainly were, were very relaxed days, with none of the pressures of business that I have to face now.'

The hardest part of working, for Anni-Frid, was being away from her children for long stretches. She said later: 'I miss them very much and it hurts me to be forced to leave them for so long, but I see them as much as I can, and we really get on well together. Fortunately, they have a good father in Ragnar, and they are very happy.'

Ragnar, for his part, was very understanding. He said: 'I am not afraid of playing second fiddle to Anni-Frid's career. If she has the chance to be successful, she must take it. I would never stand in her way.' Leaving the children behind was an awfully big wrench for her. Everybody could see the sadness in her eyes when she spoke about being away from them.

Despite her unhappiness about leaving the children, Anni-Frid felt she must go and live in Stockholm to spend her time at the hub of the music business if she was to further her career. So she said goodbye to her husband and two children, leaving them in the old wooden villa they had shared, and took the train the seventy miles to Stockholm. There, she found a small flat and settled into a life which, outside working hours, meant a lot of loneliness. She said later: 'Nobody knows the strain I was under at this time. I'd present a public image of a smiling, happy singer. But underneath, I felt a lot of sadness. I'm sorry to say that many people who should have known better were very nasty about what I had done. They said I didn't care about my children, and abandoned them to come to Stockholm to work with the big boys. They could not have been more wrong. I had not abandoned them. In fact, I thought of bringing them to Stockholm with me. Then I looked round my tiny flat and realised that that was a silly thought. There was no room, and I would not have been able to look after them properly. I did the right thing. Ragnar looked after them well and they were better off with him than stuck in a poky little place in the big city with me. I tried not to think about missing them, but it was very hard. I tell you, I shed quite a few tears over them in those days.'

Although Anni-Frid thought the world of her children, her marriage to Ragnar was not a very good one. She really thought she was doing the best thing for the children. So it was really the combination of a marriage going off the boil and a career hotting up which made her leave them. She was so upset that people said such unpleasant things about her going away. The authors believed her when she said: 'It is very hard for me to do it, but I can leave the children because I know they will have a better time with their father than with me.' Her decision did mean that she got into the mainstream of Swedish showbusiness and she completed a very full apprenticeship.

This took Anni-Frid through the full course of appearances in restaurants, melody festivals, and reviews. Her records sold well and she became a regular visitor to the Swedish best-selling charts, though the knockers claimed that her singing appealed to only a narrow audience. She got the opportunity to work with many of the most popular artistes and actors in Scandinavia, and she took part in international song contests around the world, including two in Japan and Venezuela. Appearances on the popular Swedish Television programme 'Hyland's Corner' ensured her nationwide recognition and set her firmly on the road to becoming, in her own right, one of Sweden's premier singers.

CHAPTER TWO

# BENNY

If anybody asks the jovial, bearded, and ever-so-slightly rotund Benny Andersson about his education, he has a smiling and ready reply for them. 'I have a driver's licence,' he says. It is his benign cover for a schooling that never got on the move, let alone reached the dizzy heights. The only subject he could handle with any ability was English, which, in stark contrast to the other subjects, he absorbed like a sponge. But his consuming interest in life was, and still is, music. Not that he can read music. Like other academic subjects, that is too much like hard work, and the written theory is a continuing mystery to him. Music to him meant playing: playing anything he could lay his hands on – an accordion, harmonica, whatever came his way. He was fortunate in having a father and grandfather who both had a musical bent and were determined to cultivate the budding talent in young Benny. They did so by giving him a piano-accordion.

Born in the suburbs of Stockholm, on 16 December, 1946, Benny drifted through his school life with the air of sleepy detachment which has so often characterized him when he comes up against something he is not really interested in. He left school at fifteen without taking any of the leaving examinations and settled down to concentrate full time on music. The mysteries of the accordion were soon overcome by his inquisitive musical fingers, and he progressed to a piano which was brought into the house as a further encouragement to him.

Benny recalls: 'I think coming from a musical family gives you something in life that everybody else should feel envious of. My grandfather and father were just like me. They would try any, but *any*, musical instrument that they could find, whether it was the piano-accordion they gave me, or a flute, or a fiddle. I guess I just inherited whatever they had. They loved folk music, the older and cornier the better. I learned a lot of the old tunes from them and my early playing had a definite folk flavour about it. I'm glad to say that is all in the past now.'

He was two years out of school and still trying to decide which part of the business world would benefit from his presence before any outsider recognised the talent which his family had known was there from the very beginning. The meantime had been filled in with musing about the future and playing piano with a group whose name has long since drifted into the annals of anonymity. But it was his membership of this group which was to lift him from the doldrums and plant him where his ability could be used. The group had to travel to an engagement, and as this was unusual – no-one normally *asked* them along – they had to look around for someone with the transport to get them to their rare playdate. Their thoughts lit upon Svenne Hedlund, a singer with a group called Hep Stars, who was the proud possessor of a sizeable van. Svenne was free that night and agreed to drive them in his van, which was old but vast, and perfect for the task of carrying a group and their mountain of equipment. Svenne stayed to watch the show, and saw immediately that Benny was head and shoulders above his partners. Shortly after, Hep Stars lost their organ player and Svenne's thoughts returned to Benny. He asked Benny, who accepted with alacrity, realising that his first group was on that short slide into oblivion.

Svenne peers back into the past to recount: 'Benny was a good musician, but he wasn't like the rest of us in Hep Stars at all. He had neat crewcut hair and wore a tie. He was so clean and nice. We all had long hair, and looked a pretty wild lot. And we thought ties were for wearing at funerals. But I'll give it to Benny. He made the transformation in a few months. He grew his hair long and looked as wild as the rest of us.'

With the twin sex-appeal power of Svenne and Benny in the van, Hep Stars became the biggest rock group in Sweden, in fact the biggest pop music happening in that country till Abba came along. Benny remembers: 'When I look back at Hep Stars, I realise we used to play a sort of country and western with a German beat, if you can imagine that. At the time, though, we thought we were an up-to-the-minute rock group; and luckily that's what everybody else seemed to think we were.'

Benny was looked upon as the newcomer to the group for a long time by the other four members, who had all been in on the founding of Hep Stars. It didn't worry him, as long as he could play. As always, Benny just seemed to be floating through life. He was always laughing and joking and always, but always, seemed so content. Nothing worried him and he didn't seem to have it in him to be able to get angry. When everybody else in Hep Stars was getting uptight and gritting their teeth, he would be sitting there, calm as an old man on a park bench. All the problems of the group just passed straight over his head and it was as if he didn't even notice they were there. And the group had plenty of problems. They drove the recording technicians mad because they were pathologically incapable of getting to a recording studio together and on time. Often, they were hours late because some of them had overslept. Then they would argue backwards and forwards, and shout and scream about whether a number should be done this way or that. And in the middle of it all, the unruffled Benny would be playing a gentle tune on his harmonica. He just had to be seen to be believed.

Hep Stars moved from playing youth clubs around Stockholm to jet into a bigger orbit. Their following built up quickly, they started getting bookings up and down the country and, suddenly, they were stars, looked upon as Sweden's answer to The Beatles. Which they weren't. But it was a comforting title to carry, even if the bank manager was totally unimpressed. Their tours started taking in the open-air theatres of the *folkparks* during the short but sweet Swedish summer. Their crossover into more adventurous pop music coincided with a rise in their earnings. But Benny never seemed interested in money. All he wanted out of life was to play music, and he was now getting plenty of opportunity to do that, so he was delighted. The earnings from his work have always seemed secondary to Benny. Benny would play for the rest of his life for no money. He's the sort of person who is addicted to instruments. If there is one around, he'll be there, playing it. He turned up at hotels on working tours and went straight to the piano to knock out a tune. It wouldn't matter to him that he was going to spend the rest of the night working on a piano. And if Benny is missing suddenly from a party or company, you know where he has gone. Find the musical instrument in the house, and you'll find him.

Not long after Benny teamed up with Hep Stars, they were putting a bunch of tunes together to make a long playing record, but found that they were one short. None of them could think of a suitable tune to fit in the last slot. Benny saved the day after he came up to Svenne to quietly whisper, in a most unselfconfident manner: 'I've written a song, and I think we can use.'

'I hope we can,' said Svenne. 'It could be just what we need.' It was. The song was 'No Response', which was truly a misnomer, because it was a very big 1965 hit for Hep Stars.

However, this success did not transform Benny into a bundle of energy. 'In fact, when it came to knuckling down to work, he was bordering on the lazy,' said Svenne. 'We had to wait a long time before he came up with another song for us. Strange that he seemed to be playing music all the time, which was such a joy to him that it wasn't like work. But when it needed some concentration and some effort to put a song together, it was always something he was going to get round to later.'

Benny did eventually write more for Hep Stars, and turned out many of their hits of the 1960s. In fact, two of his songs, 'Wedding', which he wrote with Svenne Hedlund, and 'Sunny Girl' were instrumental in enhancing the reputation of the group. By the time he was nineteen he had written just three tunes in his life, but they had all got into the song charts, and two of them were in the top ten at the same time. 'Wedding' went to number one.

His method of songwriting has not changed over the years. First he would tinkle about on the piano until he found some chords that pleased him. Then he'd string them together to complete the melody. When that was done, his imagination would go walkabout to search for lyrics which matched the mood of the music. 'Wedding' got its title because Benny thought the opening bars were like the church music he had heard at weddings. 'That's because it starts out like a church organ,' he said. 'I played it to a church organist who thought it sounded like a wedding march. So I wrote the lyric about a wedding. And, although English isn't my native language, I find writing in it easy enough if I have something to write about.' His next step was to get someone to write the notes down for him; this is something he still has to do for, even now, he has not learned to write music.

Benny quickly established himself as the most talented musician in the group. He also rapidly challenged Svenne Hedlund as the sex symbol of the group, the one their growing band of screaming teenagers shoutest loudest for. This was because Benny looked shy and nice and had that generous smile.

Benny was, and is, modest and gentle and loveable, a big, warm, cuddly guy. But he did like being an idol for the teenagers and all the adulation that went with it. What he didn't like about it was that it restricted his second favourite hobby – going to restaurants. They couldn't go openly to a restaurant, because they would be mobbed. So he and Svenne indulged themselves with big American cars, and it became a familiar sight to see them turn up separately and make a dash into the concert hall, avoiding the flesh-tearing clutches of the fans.

When he wasn't doing one of those lightning dashes, Benny was his usual lethargic self. A friend recalls: 'Whenever I called him when he was on tour, he was in bed. He always seemed to be tired.' He teamed up with a songwriter called Lars Berhagen to write more hit songs for Hep Stars, who by now were winning one gold record after another and chalking up 100,000 sales of individual records – very high totals for Sweden in those days. Said Benny: 'It's easier for two to write a song, especially if you are a bit lazy. You can push each other along.' Lars Berhagen, playing the guitar to Benny's piano, certainly had a remarkable method of keeping Benny on the right track. If Lars didn't like what he was playing, he would go up and bang the piano lid down on his fingers. Amazingly, Benny remembers: 'We met each other every day for a year without getting angry at each other.' The melodies were still coming easily to Benny, but he was having the usual struggle to find the lyrics. Once, he and Lars wrote what they thought would be a big smash hit for Cilla Black. Unfortunately, she never got round to hearing it.

The Hep Stars began their own publishing and business company to exploit and market the songs they were writing. They also had grandiose plans to publish other people's music and make their records. The company was called Hep House, and it was the biggest flop Benny has ever been associated with.

When Benny had just started in pop music, it was for fun. Only when the tunes he wrote in his happy-go-lucky way became successful did he take the business more seriously. Up until then he had just been fooling around. Looking at the track record of Hep House, it is clear that Benny would have been better off tackling pop in his old, nonchalant way. Hep House showed the pop stars that they were amateurs in business. They lost their money faster than they made it. They invested in the production of a film which was to be made in Africa, but not an inch of film was shot. They paid for a trip to America, for reasons which no-one now can quite remember. They also were induced to hire a private plane to take them to London, on the promise that a recording there would inject the 'British sound' and new life into their music. But there was no mystical secret to be found in that basement Soho studio. The record was never released.

At the end of this foray into big business, Benny was much

wiser, but also much poorer. The company went bankrupt, leaving Benny with a monumental tax bill to meet on his earlier earnings. He was to earn virtually nothing from the next few songs he wrote because the taxman's demands were always on the doormat.

A problem of a different nature was waiting for Benny. In the summer of 1966 he had broken off a four year engagement to Christina Grönvall, a pretty red-haired girl he had met at school. They had lived together most of that time and Christina bore him two children, a boy called Peter, and a girl, Helena. The romance had been a closely guarded secret because these were the days when it was considered anathema for news of a pop star's girlfriend to get out. A few months after the break-up, Christina challenged him in a Swedish magazine article: 'Tell them about me and the kids, the family you don't have room for in the glittery world of a pop idol.' She said Benny had left their flat at Valingby, near Stockholm, and the only contact the children had had with their father since then was through the Hep Stars records. Christina said: 'He ended our engagement very quickly. Just one phone call. No explanations.' Benny kept quiet about her and the children, she said, because he did not want his fans to find out. 'His fans would be jealous and Benny thought this would damage his career,' said Christina. 'To go around with a baby carriage in his company was unthinkable. Once I followed the Hep Stars on tour, but I had to travel behind in the orchestra bus and hide during the show.' But some fans knew about the relationship. The telephone rang one night just after Christina had put the children to bed. A girl's voice asked for Benny, but Christina said he was away on tour. The girl asked who she was talking to and Christina told the girl her name. A minute later the girl telephoned again. This time she was hysterical. When Christina answered, she screamed: 'Keep away from Benny.' Benny would not discuss the relationship at the time, but he has talked about it to friends, and made it clear he was shocked that people should take such an avid interest in his personal affairs. This sort of thing is common in Sweden, where couples live together often for many years before they marry. Sometimes they break up, and the girl is left to look after one or two children on her own. Benny told friends he was surprised so much fuss was made about it. He was also disappointed that people wanted to pry into a part of his life which he considered private and entirely his own business. He still feels that way.

CHAPTER THREE

# BJORN

Bjorn Ulvaeus started a folk singing quartet with a bunch of school friends to while away the time until he went to college. It was just an exercise in fun for him, but his proud mother thought she was witnessing the birth of a musical miracle. She dreamed up a name for the group and, without telling them, entered the boys for a radio talent contest. They didn't win, but listening to the show was a man whose instant belief in the four youngsters would project them, within the space of a few weeks, into the mainstream of Swedish showbusiness.

During the dying days of the Second World War, Bjorn was born on 25 April, 1945, in the west coast city of Gothenberg. When he was eleven years old, his family moved to the tiny and beautiful east coast town of Vastervik – a name meaning 'West Bay' in English. He learned to play the guitar fooling around with a group playing skiffle, the raw folk music which was sweeping the world at that time. At seventeen, Bjorn called three of his musical pals together and told them he wanted to form a Dixieland jazz band. The idea was to play dates to raise money for the school. Now he admits: 'It wasn't really a very serious undertaking, though I think I managed to give some people the impression that it was. For my part, I wanted something to get involved in while I was waiting to go to college. My talk to the guys about jazz and all that stuff was a bit ostentatious. I didn't know much about it, and our music came out more like American folk music, in the style of the Kingston Trio, who were a very big group then. I'm not sure if we realised it at the time, but we were probably copying them.' Whatever the source of their style, the people of Vastervik liked them, and the boys stayed together. Then, one day their practice sessions at Bjorn's home stirred his mother to fill in a form, entering them for an 'Opportunity Knocks' style programme on Swedish Radio, the government-run equivalent of the BBC. The form requested the name of the performers, but the group at that time had no name. So the inventive Mrs Ulvaeus borrowed the English versions of their town name to write in 'The West Bay Singers'.

'I was astonished when I heard she had entered us,' says Bjorn. 'At first I wanted to withdraw us from the contest, because I was in no way sure that we were ready for that sort of thing. Then I reconsidered. I thought: "Why shouldn't we be in it? We're not that bad. We might have a chance. Who knows?" And the name had a pleasant folksy ring about it, which matched the style of our performance, where we sang most of our songs in unison. I told the others about the entry, and they showed none of my reserve. They thought it was a great idea to compete.'

A review of the programme, mentioning that The West Bay Singers were entered, and that they would be singing in both Swedish and English, appeared in a newspaper read by Bengt Bernhag, a prolific discoverer of Swedish talent. He was a wise old cat who had that uncanny knack of spotting the potential of performers which more suave, but less intuitive, competitors lacked. He produced a couple of girl singers who no-one else had been prepared to do anything for. They became chart-toppers. He launched an old trumpet player who specialised in folk music. Everybody in the business laughed – especially Bengt when the trumpeter's records were big hits. He always managed to have the last laugh, but he never rubbed his successes in. He was ever the self-effacing, modest, and polite, and carefully disguised dynamo. Bengt liked the name 'The West Bay Singers', and resolved to listen to the radio show. He found he also liked the simple, honest and straightforward presentation of the group. He mentioned the group to the boss of his organisation, an irreverent, establishment-rocking, and energetic music publisher and producer, Stikkan Andersson. They contacted Bjorn to ask for a demonstration tape. This came up to expectations, so Bengt and Stikkan asked the group to come up to their Stockholm studios for a more precise and exacting test. They sailed through this, with Bengt's and Stikkan's approval registering in their beaming faces.

Bjorn recalls: 'That was a very nervous day for all of us, believe me. From a nowhere, nothing, group doing schoolboy gigs we were suddenly under the searching gaze of two of the best pros in the music business. But their calm manner in dealing with us – they must have realised we would be very much on edge – helped to cool us down and we played and sang well that day.'

The first thing Stikkan Andersson did for the group was to change their name. The American Hootenanny music was starting to emerge and looked like being the new worldwide rage. For a while he'd carried the name for a group, which he was about to present to Bjorn and his friends. It was 'The Hootenanny Singers'. Not that their music was even remotely Hootenanny. It was just a commercial, infectious, and memorable name which Stikkan was convinced would help them. Stikkan said recently: 'The West Bay name was nice, but very parochial and olde worlde. Not the sort of title for a group of young guys who, I felt sure, were going to hammer their way into the charts.'

So 'The Hootenanny Singers' they became, and Bjorn recalls the irony of that decision. 'A few weeks before we didn't even have a name,' he said. 'Then my Mum – good old Mum, it all happened because of her and I often find myself saying a few silent words of thanks to her – picked our first name. It was that name which drew the attention of Bengt and got us into the studios. And the next thing is we were given a new name for our first recording. Strange, but that's just the way it was.'

First record for The Hootenanny Singers was a perfect foil for their melancholy unison singing. It carried the wordy and strange title of 'I'm Waiting at the Charcoal Kiln' and was a sad old Swedish song about people who worked in the forest.

Immediately it was a success. Exhilarating for the boys and a memorable moment for Stikkan Andersson; he had just launched his own label, Polar Records, and Hootenanny were the first artistes to go out on that label. Said Stikkan: 'I felt the group had good potential, if they got the right guidance. They blended so well and the blond, good-looking Bjorn was a natural, and a great lead for them. But an immediate smash success was more than any of us had dared hope for.'

In 1964, with his college aspirations temporarily shelved, Bjorn and The Hootenanny Singers went on tour around Sweden, including the inevitable *folkparks*. 'At the time those *folkparks* tours seemed the hardest of all,' says Bjorn. 'The conditions for the artistes were appalling, and we were on the move all the time. But, in retrospect, I think we learned a lot and the tours did afford us the pleasure of seeing all of the country.' The Hootenanny Singers quickly built up a solid following amongst both teenagers and older people. 'We didn't get mobbed or anything like that, but that sort of idolisation I can do without,' says Bjorn.

After a year on tour, Bjorn got the feeling that perhaps the other members of the group were not as dedicated to making a musical career as he was. They started doing odd jobs, working in their father's firms, doing book-keeping, or selling cars. The truth was that the other members of the group were essentially small-town boys who were a little frightened by the sudden success. Bjorn, on the other hand, quickly outgrew the small-town mentality. If he goes back to Vastervik now, he feels a stranger. So Bjorn started to have his doubts about his own showbusiness career and took up his place at the University of Stockholm to read Economics and Law. This phase was not to last long. He did not seem to take university life so seriously. He was always hopping from one course to another, as if he could not make up his mind where to settle. His heart was really in the music business and he used to say he thought he could make it as an international artiste. But he felt he should hedge his bets by studying at the University in case the group fell apart. The courses were easy for him. He was always a bit of an intellectual, and had excelled in most subjects at school.

The stirring confidence of Stikkan Andersson and the fatherly advice of Bengt Bernhag persuaded Bjorn where his future lay. Stikkan told him that since starting his music business, he had determined that one day he would break out of the straitjacket of limitations which faced most people in the business in Sweden. He was going to launch an international star, he confided. And that star he felt sure was Bjorn.

Bjorn could not have fallen into a better set-up to assure his future. Bengt was a great music technician, and taught him all he knew. In fact, he always looked on Bjorn as his son. Which, in a way, he was. For without Bengt, Bjorn superstar might never have been created. And Stikkan showed him the business end of things, something Bjorn took to like a duck to water. A friend says: 'Stikkan has always been a businessman *par excellence*, and the only mind I have met that I think could ever make a match for him is Bjorn's. He is a cold and analysing type of person. If you watch him when he is working on business or the production of a record, you can almost hear his mind ticking over, just like a precision machine. Why, he is so mechanical, he even has to remind himself to smile on-stage.'

The Hootenanny Singers went back on tour, and they were to stay together as a group for years, turning out a considerable number of hits on the way. However, they were not wealthy enough to travel in style yet. An old Volvo with their double bass strapped on top was the sign that they had arrived in town. Even the car didn't belong to the group. They had to borrow that from one of their fathers.

Bjorn always stood out in the group; he was always the anchor man. Bengt Bernhag picked out songs which he could make as a solo artiste, a career which he nurtured while Bjorn was still with The Hootenanny Singers. He gave up the University, and dedicated himself to his music career.

He knew The Hootenanny Singers were a limited commodity. Three guys playing guitars and the other a bass while they sing folksy music was not the sort of presentation he could see going onto the world's stage. So he pitched his single-minded and absolute determination into soaking up everything he could about the business and production end, and at the same time made a number of solo records. He used to say that he didn't think The Hootenanny Singers could last, but that he wanted to be sure to be around when they had gone. He was determined to carve himself a long career in the music business. But he did not have just a limited Swedish career in mind. From the very early days he wanted to be a big international name. He really believed that Swedish music and artistes could make it abroad. He would say: 'It hasn't happened before because no-one has really tried. I'm convinced it can be done, and that I can do it.'

That's what Bjorn has – a lot of confidence. Add to that the facts that he is a planner and organiser, with a fantastic capacity for work, and you have a formidable combination. He has his eyes wide open for the faintest glimmer of an opportunity, and when one presents itself, he grabs it with an iron grip.

The Hootenanny Singers continued on the success trail, with their family audiences enjoying their clean-cut college-group air. But, businesslike and cool as he may be offstage, all the sex appeal of the group centred on Bjorn. He was the one the girls went for.

Bjorn was no shrinking violet. When a journalist asked him who was the musical brain behind the group, he immediately replied: 'I am.' Though he did give the other members of the group some credit for consultation. He candidly admitted the problems of four musicians trying to work together, adding: 'We are learning to handle that as we get more experienced. And we are pals, working pals, and because we care about each other, it helps.' Their success, he was also honest enough to admit, did not depend on them being the best musically. 'The most important thing is that we choose the right songs to go with our style,' he said. 'We sing as simply as we can. We have a distinctive combined voice, and it is that which makes us identifiable to people.'

Bowing to public demand, The Hootenanny Singers drifted from folk music to pop. They started singing all their songs in English, which is the international language for pop. 'And, anyway, the kids think songs in Swedish must be old fashioned,' said Bjorn. 'So what can we do? They are the customers, after all. The *folkparks* customers seem to be getting younger and younger all the time, and if it is pop they want, pop it is they'll get. I'm not much on looking into the future, but I do wonder what we'll be doing a few years from now.'

CHAPTER FOUR

# AGNETHA

Little Gerhard was a pop singer who retired gracefully into the role of A & R man. Like all of his colleagues around the world, he is regularly plagued by people who would like him to listen to their sister, daughter, or wife's brother. This time it was his cousin. She was singing with a dance band and wanted to make a record. Gerhard asked her to tape one of her shows and send him the tape, which he promised to accord his undiluted attention. The tape duly arrived and Gerhard dutifully sat through all of it. He called up his cousin to say: 'I'm sorry, but I don't think most of that was very good.' However, there was a glimmer of hope. 'I noticed a few snatches of song which were quite good,' he said. 'Why don't you record those songs fully, and I'll listen to them. If you sing like that all the time, I think we can do something.'

There was not a crumb of comfort in this for the cousin. She had to explain: 'But the voice singing those short pieces is not mine. That's a new girl we have singing with the band.' Exit the crestfallen cousin and enter the new girl – the diminutive, blonde, and pretty Agnetha Faltskog.

Agnetha's father, an enthusiastic amateur entrepreneur, used to stage shows in their home town, the lakeside Jonkopping, where she was born on 5 April, 1950. At a tender age, she was introduced to the boards, to sing a song in one of the amateur revues for a gathering of local old folk. 'I shall never forget that start to my career,' she has recounted. 'In the middle of of the song my knickers fell down and the whole of the audience collapsed in hysterical laughter. I was six years old.'

Undaunted by this inauspicious opening, she spent hour after hour with her father and grandfather, playing the family accordion and piano. When she was ten she was given her own piano and very soon she was picking out the notes, concocting her own melodies. She also wrote words to go with the music, beginning with a revue sketch about two trolls – kind Nordic monsters. She returned to the amateur revues to enrapture the audience which had earlier found her so funny. By the time she was fifteen, Agnetha was the regular singer with a dance band orchestra in Jonkopping – looking, despite her age, every inch an accomplished professional. Two years later, she started appearing as the 'guest singer' with other dance bands in the area which is how her voice got on to the tape that ended up in Little Gerhard's office.

Gerhard, an executive with the CBS-Cupol record company, called Agnetha and asked her to send a full tape of one of her songs to him. Her favourite song at that moment was 'I Was So In Love', a heavily sentimental song about a girl who had just lost the big love of her life. That girl was her. She had written the song because she felt so unhappy when her romance with a local boy, Bjorn Lilja, was broken off. She remembers: 'I sat down at the piano and started to play, just to try to forget how unhappy I felt. Half an hour later the melody was finished. I didn't feel any better, but I had what I thought was a lovely and moving song.' Little Gerhard agreed with her opinion. He asked her to come to Stockholm to make a record of her song. So the tiny and nervous Agnetha was put on the train which would take her to the ancient and beautiful capital city of Sweden, which for all Swedes has the simple and reverent title of 'the town'. Her father was there to see her off, with a few final words of advice, and her mother, with a little flutter of concern for her baby daughter. She need not have worried. Agnetha was to prove a formidable match for the big boys of the record world.

She vividly remembers walking into the recording studio for the first time. 'It was the most exciting moment of my life,' she said. 'My heart was in my mouth and I had to consciously make my feet take the steps down to the recording room. Then I heard the string musicians practising my music, the very notes I had picked out on that piano. Suddenly, I was walking on air and floated into the room as if I was on a cloud.'

Little Gerhard was delighted with the two tapes the recording session produced. His boss was somewhat less pleased. He asked him what he thought he was doing wasting the company's time and money on taping a girl from the country who was a complete unknown. When he heard the tapes, he changed his tune. Agnetha was called up to his office, and she immediately sat down to negotiate her own contract. He must have been amazed to find such a tough mind in that tiny, delicate frame. Despite the fact that she was a total newcomer and only seventeen, she was one of the first artistes to have a guaranteed income clause. It gave her a monthly salary for the next three to five years for making records and doing tours.

Within two weeks of release, 'I Was So In Love' was number one on the record charts. Agnetha, who gave up her job as a switchboard operator for a car sales firm and moved to a flat in Stockholm, said: 'I never imagined, that day I sat down to play a few bars of self-condolence, that anybody else would even hear the music. Then a year later it was in the charts. Unbelievable! My boyfriend and I never did patch up our differences, but we are still friends. And I am very grateful to him. If it had not been for him, and if I had not been so unhappy that day, I would never have written that song.' Bjorn Lilja, for his part, was ecstatic about Agnetha's success, and he felt proud that he had inspired the song. He went to see her to offer his congratulations. He wanted to hug her, too, but could not. He had broken both his arms in an accident, and they were in plaster.

Her father, who had already helped her career so much, continued to do so by taking over her business affairs and acting as her manager. She said of him: 'I owe him so much. His patience in spending hours and hours with me at the piano and his continual encouragement have done so much to help me to where I am today. I'll never forget what he did for me.'

From the start, Agnetha developed a reputation as a forceful and highly individual and opinionated girl. The most galling thing about her, to the old established musicians, was that she was usually right. Little Gerhard recalls: 'Right from the start, she was very outspoken about songs, including her own. She said what she thought and she always knew what she wanted. She could recognise a good song if she heard one, and she always knew instinctively if a song would be right for her. Even in those early days, at seventeen years of age, she could listen to a tape once and decide immediately whether she wanted to sing a certain song or not. She had an incredibly wise head on her young shoulders.'

'I Was So In Love' was a gushing, oversentimental song, expressing the high emotional sentiments of a young girl. A strong emotional tension ran through most of her songs, though she once protested: 'Why does everyone think I can only sing about love and that sort of thing? I really can sing other music, too. But songs will always be about love. New and old, it's all alike. It's always like that. I write my love songs under the influence of two flickering candles on my piano. They bring out the romance in me.' Despite her reservations about supercharged emotion in her songs, the Swedish people took her and her music to their hearts. Her two follow-up songs, 'Without You' and 'If Tears Were Gold', were as sentimental as her first – and as successful. She wrote and sang romantic songs because she was a romantically-minded girl, and this just happened to click with the sort of music the public were looking for at that time.

Her forthright manner was to make her social transition from a country town to Stockholm difficult. Despite her apparent bluff self-confidence, she was hiding an inherent shyness. In fact, much of her manner was caused by this. It made her say things she did not mean and she often appeared rude. A friend remembers her early days in Stockholm. 'She had no manners at all, and made all the social *faux pas* you can imagine. She could not even handle a spoon properly. And she was forever saying and doing the wrong things. I remember a time when she was having dinner in a restaurant with some music company people and she embarrassed everybody at the table by shouting at the waiter, complaining about the food, and using coarse language. I'm sure she didn't realise what she was doing, and that the words only tumbled out because she was feeling so shy and insecure. For when she talked to people in private, she was so nice, sweet, and honest. I think that in company she felt so awkward that she overcompensated by being rude and loud. I understand that now she drives interviewers mad. They can't get more than a simple "Yes" or "No" out of her. I think she finally learned that it was better to say nothing than put her foot in it all the time. But she makes up for her public silence in private conversation, when she seems to talk all the time.'

None of this hindered her career, which flowered unchecked. She started appearing on television and set off on the inevitable *folkparks* tours. She included in her growing repertoire 'One Summer With You', which her father had written, and made a special tour to the schools in the Jonkopping area, singing the children a song she had penned about the correct way to brush their teeth. A German record company heard her records, and tried to get her under contract. She turned the offer down, but her popularity in Germany grew, and for a short while she was engaged to a German songwriter, Dietrich Zimmerman. They wrote a number of songs together, but their romance died.

She announced plans to start an acting career, but while she was still making hit records, it was hard for her to take it up. One of her hits, a song called 'Gipsy Friend', which she also wrote herself, was criticised as being racial because it told of the old legends about gipsies. She said: 'I'm sorry if that's what people think. I was only writing a song, that's all.' But she reverted to the sentimental love songs which the public still loved, and which kept her out of the hot water of barbed criticism.

CHAPTER FIVE

# A MR BIZ

So the cast was prepared. Four young people, each with their own particular musical ability, were all doing well enough in their own way. But alone they were not going to set the world on fire. Pop experts remember The Beatles in much the same way on the threshold of their career. To light The Beatles' fuel, a torch was needed. He came along, in the form of Brian Epstein, to manage them and ensure their musical immortality. For Anni-Frid, Benny, Bjorn and Agnetha, another such catalyst was waiting in the wings, like a fairy godmother who was going to transform their lives. He was Stikkan Andersson, a former schoolmaster with an impressive zest for business and hard work.

Stikkan Andersson is particularly proud of the fact that he has struggled up to a successful career from a fatherless childhood. His mother was unmarried, a fact that any modern Swede would shrug off as of absolutely no consequence. But in the tiny village of Hova, set in the countryside near Gothenberg, in 1931, long before the sexually enlightened times of post-war Sweden, it was a heavy burden. He felt like an underdog, and claims that this was the prime driving force which made him work hard and determined him to succeed in life. He got an after-school-hours job as a messenger when he was thirteen to save up the money to buy a guitar. Then, as soon as he could play it, he used it to earn more money playing with local dance bands. At fifteen he left school, and immediately started writing songs. His objective? To earn enough money to go to college and train for the career he had set his heart on – as a teacher. He also started writing songs, though, as a self-taught musician, he could not write down the music. When he was eighteen he got his first song published. It went over in a small way, but it was a start and encouraged him to beaver away at more. He wrote a number of comedy songs and included them in a repertoire he built up for tours around the Swedish *folkparks*. Then he teamed up with a friend and for a while they toured as a comedy-singing double act. When Stikkan had saved enough money, he went to college to study and qualify as a teacher, but still managed stage appearances in the evenings. After graduation he got a job teaching chemistry and mathematics in a Stockholm secondary school. Even then, he still spent the evenings writing songs and making occasional appearances.

The end of his teaching career was spelled out by a song he wrote called 'Are You Still In Love With Me, Klas-Goran?' A popular Swedish singer, Lil-Babs, recorded it in 1960 and won a gold record. Stikkan made a lot of money out of it, and realised he could have a big future in showbusiness. He now recalls: 'I enjoyed working at the school, and I had devoted a lot of time and effort to get there. I would rather have done that than stay in small time showbusiness. But if I could get into the really commercial end of the business, who was I to refuse? The music had, anyway, seemed to be getting progressively more important to me, so it was a natural transition. However, it is amusing to look back to see that I concentrated on music to get me through college, and that it was the music which finally took me away from my teaching. That's the way of things, I suppose. What happens in life that you have planned carefully beforehand? Not much.'

All of Stikkan's earlier songs had been published by someone else, and there had been a few minor sellers among them. The 'Klas-Goran' song was something different. It was his first big song, and he used it as the basis of setting himself up as a music publisher. This business he set up in his small house, and he left the school to run it.

From the start, Stikkan was like a breath of fresh wind to music publishing in Sweden. He had a lot of new ideas and boundless energy to carry them out. Swedish publishing at that time was very calm and unruffled and conventional. Publishers sat around, waiting for songs to come in from abroad, then passed them on to artistes to record. It was a very sleepy way of going on: how to fail in business without really trying. Stikkan wrote hundreds of letters to people abroad, offering to translate their songs into Swedish and market them here. And while he was doing all this, he was still writing his own original lyrics at night. He was fresh, he worked like a slave, and slowly he got himself a bigger and bigger slice of the music cake. He is a human dynamo, and some years he was translating four or five hundred lyrics. It got so that it seemed every song played on Swedish Radio he had something to do with. This only encouraged him to write more and more. His best-ever record was writing six of the lyrics in the Swedish top ten. He was phenomenal, and it was not just a matter of churning out anything and some of it being successful by the natural law of averages. He really had a good nose for a potential hit.

Like most successful men, Stikkan built up a stable of enemies, and a considerable number of critics. He was totally outspoken and very controversial. Journalists got to know that a call to Stikkan Andersson would guarantee them some material which ranged from the nonconformist to the outrageous. One illustrious phrase has remained in people's memories, and is constantly coming back to haunt him. Talking about the popular music on the scene at the time, he said: 'People are not as dumb as we think. They are dumber.' He also raised many a laugh and established his eccentricity over his name. His birth certificate name is Stig, and Stikkan the nickname. Now, everybody else in Sweden who uses the nickname spells it Stickan. That was not good enough for Stikkan. He wanted to be different, and insisted on it being spelt with two Ks. Whenever he was interviewed by a journalist, he made a point of telling them how his name was spelt. It became a gimmick with him.

None of this did anything to stunt the growth of his company, which he had eloquently dubbed 'Sweden Music'. It was soon worthy of the title. The songs flowed in from all over Europe and his pen was never still. In the 1960s he had more hits in Sweden than anybody else, and by 1965 he estimated that he had written the lyrics of more than 3,000 songs.

Stikkan, who, with his moustache and abbreviated beard, still carries the studious and intent looks of a schoolmaster, recalls his struggles with a certain relish. He said: 'All the fight of the early days was worth it. It all prepared me for the bigger battles ahead.'

Those battles were to be rigorous – and Stikkan was to come out on top. Despite his country origins, he was no small town dreamer heading for the big city, expecting to find its streets paved with gold. He knew that if he was going to find any gold, he would have to make it from his own effort and expertise. By the time his biggest challenges came along, he was already a fully-fledged businessman who knew his way around the tight corners.

There was no way a man like him was going to endear himself to the established mandarins of the music world. He was rude. He spoke out. He was unorthodox. But what they feared most was that he was good. If you've got a nice sleepy thing going, what could be a bigger shock than to find an energised talent snapping at your heels? Before Stikkan Andersson, the image of Swedish music was firmly fixed to the folksy and the old-fashioned, comfortingly harmless to the professionals abroad. He has managed to change all that – and, in his way, reversed the trend. He used a lot of strange methods to claw his way up, but everybody in the business, including those whose fingers he trod on, have to admit that they admire his ability. How can they do anything else, in the face of his success?

He is incredibly egocentric. He is not modest about his energy and ability, and he has plenty of both. He was the first to advertise his 'bigness', so to speak, in magazines like *Billboard*. He is all staring eyes and shaking hands. He can't stop himself working all the time, and he is under a constant strain, because he never learned to relax.

Any perceptive person who knew him in the early days would have seen immediately that Stikkan was marked out for the big time. He was going to succeed because he had a sort of non-intellectual view of music-making, in stark contrast to the other music people in Sweden. He was very bad news to the companies which were stuck in the socialist rut, bleating that every song had to carry a social message or it was not worth a candle. A lot of these companies maintain a strong platform within the Swedish government radio by recording music with a political message, with the lyrics spitting fire at capitalism and commercialism. Stikkan has been in confrontation with them all the years. It has been a running battle, with the controversy flowing to and fro. The socialistic-minded companies and radio have heaped a lot of criticism on the so-called commercial industry, and Stikkan has come more and more to represent that side of the business. He has been the big, bad wolf, the ugly guy, and he has been in no end of fights with the government-run radio and television companies, always making his stand against the 'intellectuals' of music. His view was clear as a bell: If you give the public what *they* want, you'll sell well. If you try to give them what you *think* they want, you'll sell next to nothing. Such thinking upset the companies. He called them ostriches. He has never tried to be diplomatic in his life, and he sees no reason why he should have to be deferential or polite to anyone. He would talk straight, and it came very naturally to him. He would say exactly what he believed, and to hell with the consequences. His ego and his self-confidence always carried him through any storms his attitude threw up.

It came as no surprise to Stikkan that he had failed to endear himself to his rivals. They thought they could slight him by devising the name 'Mr Biz'. To them, it was a term of abuse, like calling him 'Mr Nasty'. To Stikkan, it was something quite different. It is typical of him that he scooped the name up and relishes it. To him, it demonstrates his rivals' underlying, but unconfessed, respect for him, and awe of him, as a remarkably astute businessman.

It was almost inevitable that Bjorn Ulvaeus should find himself being swept into the Stikkan Andersson net. Stikkan firmly believed that he had all the necessary attributes to break out onto the international scene as a songwriter and entrepreneur. He was never short of confidence. He dreamed that one day he would find an artiste or group he would be able to fly with into the heady air of international success, when he could become the international 'Mr Biz'. The first part of that dream slotted into place when Bjorn was presented to him by his associate, the wily Bengt Bernhag. The tall, blond, slender, good-looking young man could sing well, play the guitar, and had a commanding stage presence.

Stikkan now says: 'It was the chance of that newspaper article which brought Bjorn to me. As soon as I saw him at work, I knew he had great potential. They were a good group, but this boy was outstanding even in their company.' When their first record was a success on Stikkan's just-founded record company, Polar Music, Stikkan soon started making plans for Bjorn, looking for suitable material for him, and planning carefully to cultivate his career. After a short while, he confided his dreams to Bjorn – and found a mind which was a remarkable mirror image of his own. Bjorn also had grandiose ambitions of an international career, was prepared to put any amount of work into achieving it, and showed a singlemindedness which Stikkan had only seen in himself before then. The team was formed – and if the rare combination of talent, energy, and good fortune was enough, nothing was going to stop them.

CHAPTER SIX

# BENNY AND BJORN

The Swedish pop community of the 1960s was a very small village. But the groups rarely met each other because they spent most of their time criss-crossing the country on a succession of one-nighter tours. It was only if they bumped into each other at the same motel that they might get together for a party.

Just such a chance brought Benny Andersson and Hep Stars to the motel outside Vastervik. And staying in rooms just down the hall were The Hootenanny Singers, including Bjorn Ulvaeus. It was Bjorn's home town, but he had decided to stay with the other fellows in the group. They met up in the bar in a flutter of polite introductions and handshakes. Over a few beers, they discussed the gossip of the business, exchanged a few jokes and stories. Then Bjorn and Benny, sitting quietly just to the side of the others, came round to the subject which really enthralled both of them: music. Bjorn offered a few opinions, and Benny countered with a few of his own. Suddenly all the polite chatter was gone, and they were deep in deadly and earnest discussion. Bjorn recalls: 'Listening to Benny was like listening to myself talk. I was amazed that we both had such similar ideas about music. We both felt that the performance of our groups could be improved immensely if only we were able to write all the music for them, instead of accepting music from other writers, which was adequate, but only that.' The studious, intellectual Bjorn and the warm, happy-go-lucky Benny had hit it off immediately. They liked each other personally, and they liked each other's ideas on music. It was a case of drifting but kindred souls meeting. Each had written songs for their own groups; on the spot they both said they would like to try writing songs together.

'Our only problem was where,' said Bjorn. 'So I called up my father to ask him if he knew a place in town where I could take my guitar and sound equipment and Benny could take his piano. He worked in a factory at the time and said he thought he could arrange for us to use an office there. He fixed that up, and Benny and I got our equipment together there and then. We loaded all our gear, the amplifiers and so on, into one of the band buses and carried it all into the office block. That was the only office block with any lights showing in Vastervik that night, and our partnership had begun.'

Benny produced bunches of chords from the piano while Bjorn sat on a stool a couple of feet away, searching for notes that would develope the musical themes. 'Our styles dovetailed immediately,' remembers Benny. 'We had both tried writing with other people before, but we knew that this time we had the right partner.'

They played on far into the night, getting together snatches of a song here, bits of a melody there; nothing complete, but each piece with a lot of promise. In the dawn hours, they had to clear out of the office to make way for the incoming workers, and also to go each his own way on the tours. They promised to get together again as soon as they could and finish off their night's work. They visited each other's flats in Stockholm – less than a couple of miles apart – to do so. Their first completed song was 'Isn't It Easy To Say?' which slotted into a Hep Stars LP. The next was 'Flower Of My Garden', which found its way onto another Hep Stars LP. 'Neither of us could read music, and we still can't,' says Benny. 'And we developed a very haphazard method of throwing notes at each other which just happened to work well for both of us. As soon as one of us spotted a few chords the other liked, we'd try to build on them. It's the only way we know to put a melody together, and it's always worked very well for us. The words were always the hardest part. They would come last, and we'd try to match them with the music. We'd try to sing the songs before we got the words, by fitting in gibberish syllables, until we could work out what words to use. If anybody had heard us, I'm sure they would have sent for the men in the white coats. Fortunately, the walls of those flats were pretty soundproof, so no-one else had to listen to our music in its very raw state.'

A couple of years after their first meeting, Benny decided to quit Hep Stars because he felt he could make headway outside the group as a songwriter and performer. He approached Bjorn, and suggested they could write more songs together, and perhaps even make records together. Bjorn took Benny to meet Stikkan Andersson, and asked what he thought of the idea. Stikkan recalls: 'I never had been able to understand how two such vastly different characters got along so well together, but the evidence of their closeness was in their music, which managed to be somehow both smooth and volatile. There was magic in their partnership. I said: "Sure, why not? Let's give it a try." ' So Bjorn and Benny set up Union Songs with Stikkan. The idea was that the two boys would produce the melodies, and all three, in harmony, would write the lyrics.

Partnerships, particularly musical ones, are probably the most difficult arrangements in the world to run smoothly, and keep together. The trio succeeded. Bjorn and Benny would tinker about with the notes, and when they came up with a melody, would sit down to play it on the piano and guitar, and tape it. Then they would start getting the phrases together for the lyric. They'd pass their ideas on to Stikkan, he would add his suggestions and a few lines and hand it back to them. Eventually they'd end up with a melody and lyrics. It was a haphazard arrangement, but it worked, and their songs were successful. Some they sang themselves, others they passed on to other artistes.

'We had to make demo records of these songs,' says Benny. 'You can't go round to see artistes and producers with sheet music and lyrics. You've got to be able to demonstrate to them what the songs are all about.'

Bjorn recalls: 'If we liked the sound of a melody we had

turned out, we'd take it into Stikkan's office and try it on his piano there. The astonishing thing to me is that during all our time of composing Benny and I have never quarrelled. We have gotten more critical about our writing but we haven't quarrelled. And when you think it can take us sometimes several days to come up with one single good bar, that is pretty good going. We must have a good friendship to be able to take that sort of strain.'

Bjorn is the exact opposite to Benny in many ways, but musically they could not have hit it off better. Benny is happy and easygoing, whereas Bjorn is the intellectual type, a guy who likes to analyse things, to talk a lot. He likes to be thought of as an intellectual type, and he has a very crisp and business-like approach to life. Benny, on the other hand, seems to be at pains to prove he is by no means the intellectual type, and he is not. Many people who like Benny because he is so easygoing dislike Bjorn because he can be pernicketty and cocky, as if he knows best all the time. Sound engineers don't like Bjorn around because of this; they think he's a bit highbrow and his manners put them off. But they all have to admire his ability and his tenaciousness. It was always obvious that he was going to make a lot of money; he's not greedy, but he's what Swedes call 'money smart'.

Benny and Bjorn, in conjunction with Stikkan, have gone on to become one of the most prolific hit song teams in history. They make the perfect team. Benny is the nice guy, the born musician. He loves music, in fact he lives for music. He's playing all the time. Even now, when he spots a piano, he can't resist sitting down at the stool and playing. And when he's not playing music, he's listening to it. He is happy, perhaps at his happiest, if he is left alone for hours with an old harmonica or an accordion. He'll play all day and be as happy as a sandboy. Benny is not interested in the money and all the trappings that go with it. He's a musician pure and simple, and it's the music that keeps him happy. Bjorn, on the other hand, is the clever guy and the organiser. Benny is the guy who comes up with the spontaneous musical ideas, while Bjorn is the one who puts them in order. It is he who decides, 'We'll do it this way,' or 'We'll make it that way.' He is the planner and the brains in their team, while Benny is the musician and improvisor. And capping the partnership is the expertise of Stikkan Andersson, who is the one who can pick up the threads and weave them together, and of course do the all-important marketing for them.

Bjorn and Benny realised very early on that they had to write in English if they were going to bite into the international market. Record producers were afraid of Swedish songs, they found, and it was easier to sell them songs in English. And Stikkan told them: 'If you write in Swedish, you will write for Sweden alone. If you want to write – and play – for the world, your lyrics must be in English. That's the international language of pop.'

The boys also found that the music they liked to write was what people wanted to hear. 'That's very fortunate,' says Bjorn. 'Because it makes us very commercial, and we still get a big kick out of writing. But that's the way it must always be. If your music is not from the heart, I don't think it can be any good. I don't believe it is possible to set yourself like a computer, programmed to turn out popular music. I'm sure you would only turn out material that sounded wooden and contrived.'

For Bjorn, life was a continual battle to decide whether he wanted to be a songwriter and performer, or a backroom boy in the music world, working out the studio production. He said: 'I sometimes feel I work best in the studio, and that the studio is the place where I should be. If I were forced to choose between singing or producing records, I would opt for producing. The stage is the place where I feel least comfortable. It's always a big strain for me to be "on". I can't relax on stage. When I go on, I have to think: "Smile! Smile!" But I can't do it very well. On the other hand, I think I have the right background to be a record producer. I feel that one day I will be a businessman in music, and, in fact, that is my long-term plan. I know I can't last forever as a performer.'

This willingness to get involved in the technicalities of the business has endeared him to Stikkan. They have built up a very close relationship and a good rapport. Bjorn's sharpened business senses and his aptitude for work, combined with a shrewd mind, have led to the Stockholm pop fraternity calling him 'Mini-Biz'. It's a suitable title, because he is second only to Stikkan in his will to fight for success.

Bjorn got his wish to work outside of the Hootenanny group during one winter, when their *folkparks* summer tour was over, but the change was not to get him offstage. He spent a few months guesting with Benny's group, Hep Stars. It led them to decide to try out a record together; they made an LP called 'Happiness', which got absolutely nowhere. They followed this up with a single called 'My Kind Of Girl'. It was a hit – in Japan. But nowhere else. They both made the final break with their two groups, The Hootenanny Singers and Hep Stars. Svenne Hedlund also decided to get out of Hep Stars, and that was really the end for the group. The drummer, bass player, and guitarist who were left went on to form an outfit called The Rubber Band. Benny and Bjorn were to survive the break, but the groups could not. With their lynchpins gone, their days were numbered.

The hits continued to roll out, mainly for other artistes, and one day Benny and Bjorn devised an incredible plan of action. They announced: 'Now we'll produce songs and records between nine in the morning and five at night. It will be exactly like going to the office.'

Benny said: 'I haven't had to keep regular times since I finished school, so it will be nice to have that discipline. Many people, I know, think our work is all fun and improvisation. Well, it's not always fun. We've been doing it for years and years now and we find it very tiring, working on to the midnight hours. It's the end of all that for us.'

Bjorn said: 'It can be fun, but you can't count on it. Nine times out of ten writing a song is something we manage only after a hell of a lot of sweat and work. We'll still work the same way – tossing ideas around between us. I think we've developed to the point now where we can offer each other some useful constructive criticism.' He candidly admitted: 'We don't think everything we've turned out has been a masterpiece, and there are some tunes which, in retrospect, we now would rather we had not written.' And, talking of their future plans, he said: 'We have strong ambitions to expand in this business, and we would like to do some film music. Writing a musical must be fascinating. We'd like to try that.' Bjorn betrayed his wariness of the stage when he said: 'I think we would like other artistes to sing our more ambitious material, and the simpler songs we would handle ourselves. I don't know what we will turn out with our new approach. I guess we'll have to wait and see.' Benny just shrugged his shoulders and smiled.

Their plans to go over to a nine-to-five day didn't last very long. They found that inspiration didn't necessarily come within those hours, and they were back to burning the midnight oil, Bjorn driven by his insatiable ambition, and Benny seemingly urged along only by his love of music.

CHAPTER SEVEN

# BJORN AND AGNETHA

It was one of those Sundays straight out of the Mama Cass song: the sort of slow-moving, dreary day that showbusiness performers have learned to fear. They will claim that they enjoy the day off, a day away from work, strain, and responsibility. In fact, they usually don't know what to do with themselves without all that in their lives. Bjorn Ulvaeus switched on the radio and walked across to sprawl in an easy chair, gazing out on the Manhattan-type skyline which has imposed itself on Stockholm. The pop and ballad music droned on in succession, and Bjorn wasn't really taking any notice. It was just a background to his thoughts. Then the crystal clear voice of a young girl snapped him out of his reverie. She was singing a soft, sentimental, slushy love song, just the type Bjorn could not bear. But there was something about that voice which fascinated him. He listened all through the record, enthralled. A couple of miles away, in a similar flat, Agnetha Faltskog was listening to the same record. For a different reason, she, too, was entranced. The song, 'I Was So In Love', was her composition; and the voice singing it was hers. It was a hit by now, and she still got an excited thrill to hear her own music and her own voice on the radio.

Bjorn fell in love with that voice, though he was not to meet Agnetha for some months. He bought the record, and played it over and over and over again. Bjorn now recalls: 'It was so strange. A guy with my background shouldn't like that music at all. It was just not my style. But, for some reason, the record absolutely fascinated me. It was the voice, I guess. So sweet and delicate. Yes, I suppose I fell in love with the voice. I had never heard of Agnetha before, and I had no idea what she looked like, though I felt sure she must be delicate, fragile, and lovely. Couldn't be anything else. I played the record so many times in my flat, and even took it on tour with me so I could listen to it in my room. Looking back on it now, it amazes me that I did actually fall in love with just a voice. And the very strange thing is that my vision of Agnetha turned out to be exactly right. When I did meet her, I felt as if I'd known her a long time.'

Chance was to bring them together when they were both booked to appear on a television show being taped in Gothenberg a few months later. What Bjorn did not know was that Agnetha was a keen follower of the fortunes of The Hootenanny Singers – because he was in the group. When he walked into the television studio, Agnetha, whose boldness is well concealed by her demure looks, strode up to him, and said: 'Hello. Bjorn. I've been looking forward to meeting you. I think you're the greatest, I really dig you and your music.'

Says Bjorn: 'I knew she was Agnetha, because I had seen her on some television shows. But this sort of reaction was the last thing I expected. You could have knocked me down with a feather. I had been wondering what I would say to her after all this time. She took my breath away. Just like that, she fell in love with *me*.'

Agnetha remembers: 'I had seen a lot of their group on television, and heard them many times. I liked their music, but I particularly liked their lead guitarist and singer, that fabulous Bjorn. And when I met him, he was so nice. I remember after my forward introduction, I had a good look at him, and he was better looking than I could remember from the television screen. It was so cold waiting around for the cameras to start and he took my hands in his to warm them up. And we haven't really let go of each other since.'

Within a short while, a matter of about three months, they were secretly engaged and moved into a tiny bedsitter flat in the Kungsholm area of Stockholm, overlooking the Karlsberg Canal. In the close confines of that flat, their relationship was to have its early test by fire. Agnetha is a sweet, kind girl, but when she gets angry she is a bit of a spitfire. Bjorn was to find out, and Bjorn got to be pretty good at dodging the missiles she hurled at him when they had an argument. Most people cannot bear that sort of wild reaction and temperament. But to Bjorn it just confirmed what a fascinating and interesting person she was, someone who would never bore him. Their relationship has not changed. They are very close, and they really like each other a lot, but Agnetha has got the same sort of temperament which can send her off the deep end. Once she stopped a New Year's Eve party dead by hurling a smoked herring across the room and hitting Bjorn in the face with it. There was absolute silence for a moment, then everybody started to laugh, especially Bjorn and Agnetha. It is her way of showing she cares for him; he does not mind at all, though it is the sort of affection most of us can do without.

Not surprisingly, the rumour got around that Agnetha and Bjorn were in love. It was a disappointment for both of them because they had hoped to keep their romance secret for a while. Agnetha told a newspaper: 'I can't deny it. We are together, and we are very happy. I'm sorry we couldn't have kept it quiet for a bit longer, so we could get to know each other without any outside pressures on us.'

Bjorn said: 'We've been together for two months now, and we are in love. But we haven't thought of anything serious like engagement and so on. We want to get to know each other better before we take that sort of step. We hit it off immediately, but we want to wait a while to see if we really do like each other enough, to give our relationship a test of time.'

Shortly after, they were off in separate directions, Bjorn touring with The Hootenanny Singers and Agnetha touring with her own show. She says: 'It was terrible to be apart again. Before I met Bjorn I felt I had got to know him well through seeing him on television, and admiring him from afar. Suddenly, I was back to that, and only seeing him on television. We spent a lot on telephone calls to each other, but it was not the same as being together. I missed him so much, and because of that I got a bit fed up with the touring. It wasn't the travelling about that was the trouble. I just couldn't bear being away from Bjorn.'

They got together again to slip away on a pre-engagement trip to Cyprus, the Mediterranean island which is the legendary home of Aphrodite, the ancient Greek goddess of love. 'It was such a beautiful time,' says Agnetha. 'We strolled about like any other young couple in love. We could go where we liked, with no-one recognising us, and behave just like ordinary people for a change. But it was all over too soon, and we were back to Sweden, and the touring, and missing each other.'

When they returned, the couple did manage to spend some time together working, with a couple of television appearances, singing old Swedish songs, and making their first record together.

Their engagement was officially announced in October, 1969, and was hailed by the newspapers as 'The pop romance of the year' or 'The chart-topping romance of the year'. Agnetha and Bjorn moved to a three-bedroom flat on the quiet and exclusive island of Lilla Essenger, in the centre of Stockholm. They had to tour the town's discount warehouses looking for bargains to furnish the flat. And their romance was to continue hot and heavy. They quarrelled a lot, and they had a lot of fun.

Agnetha and Bjorn also announced a decision, which seems incredible when viewed from their present working relationship. They said they had agreed they should not work together too much. Said a friend: 'I don't know if they had worked out that couples who work together as well as live together often end up hating each other, or if they had some other motive. Whichever was the reason, they only worked together on very rare occasions and toured separately. However, when they were together they still managed to fit in some blistering arguments; but these didn't seem to affect their feeling for each other. Perhaps it is their way of freeing their relationship of tension. Despite the kippers flying about, when you see them together, you know they share a deep and overwhelming love for each other. It's written on everything they say and do.'

Summer is a revelation in Sweden. With the snows melted and the grey skies chased away, the countryside is kissed by bright sunshine and caressed by crystal-clear air. It is every Swedish girl's dream to be a summer bride. Agnetha was no exception. And on 6 July, 1971, she became a summer bride, with her handsome Bjorn at her side.

Their tours of the country had become a quest for a church they wanted to marry in. For in Sweden, couples are allowed to marry in any part of the country, without the constraint of residential qualifications and the like. Said Agnetha: 'Those tours of the *folkparks* turned out to be very useful in this way. There are *folkparks* in every part of the country, so we had the chance to search everywhere for just the right sort of church. We wanted it to be one of the fine old gothic churches set in a lovely country area. Bjorn was as eager as me to find just the right place. He perhaps won't admit it, but he's every bit as much a romanticist as I am. And we found just the perfect church, a beautiful old white building in an idyllic village setting at Verum, in Skane, Sweden's most southerly province.'

Bjorn agrees: 'It got so that we were interested in where our tours would take us more for the possibility of finding churches in the area than the actual shows we were doing. We always had an eye out to see if there was one in the area that we liked.'

That year, Agnetha, Bjorn, and Benny had teamed up to tour the *folkparks* together, more as an experiment than anything else, but it was a prophetic look into the future. Said Agnetha: 'We were quite well received, but there was something slightly out of balance; we couldn't put our finger on it, but we knew there was something not quite right. But it was a lot of fun, and I was pleased to have the opportunity to spend time with Bjorn.' Their tour was on the move right up till the day before the wedding. The couple planned to take just four days off for the briefest of honeymoons, then go back on tour.

'We had contracted appearances to keep to, and we were not going to put those off for a protracted honeymoon,' said Bjorn. 'Besides, we didn't really need one. As far as I was concerned, our time together had been one long honeymoon, anyway.'

Agnetha was driven to the church in a horse-drawn open carriage, through the thousands of people who had flocked into the tiny village, for the biggest event in its history. The local police chief had to borrow officers from a neighbouring town to help him control the crowds. Three thousand people were packed into the square in which the tree-shrouded church stood. Inside the church, three hundred guests watched the ceremony.

It was a beautiful sunny day, perfect for a wedding. Agnetha looked even more beautiful than ever when she arrived in the carriage, with two girls astride the white horses pulling it. The crowd outside were mainly holidaymakers in the area; there was a mass of summer dresses and scores of children running around without shoes on. The congregation sang two old Swedish hymns. 'In This Wonderful Summertime' and the moving 'Let The Lord Look After These Two People'.

There was a special surprise waiting for them, which was also a dream come true for Benny. He was seated at the majestic church organ as Agnetha walked down the aisle. He greeted her with Mendelssohn's Wedding March, and played them out of the church with his own hit song composition 'Wedding'. Said Benny: 'Since I was a little boy, it had been my ambition to play a church organ. It's surprising how difficult it is to do it. The custodians are very careful about who they let near the organs; I was delighted when the pastor told me it would be okay. I was every bit as happy as Bjorn and Agnetha that day. Agnetha had her dream of being a summer bride come true, and I had my wish.'

The service was very short, in the clipped tradition of the Church of Sweden, and the pastor thanked the couple for doing more for his chapel than he had done in ten years, and for giving the village the brightest day in its history. He said: 'I consider it an honour that you chose my church for the ceremony, and you have given the people of this village a memory that they will treasure all their lives.'

Said Bjorn: 'It was strange to hear him thanking us like that; as far as we were concerned, the honour was ours. He had begun our marriage with a blessing and in just the way we had hoped for.'

Their vows exchanged amidst the clicking of hundreds of instamatics, the couple walked out to a rapturous greeting from the crowd, which surged forward when they appeared. So closely were they packed around the church that Agnetha was pushed against a police horse doing crowd control duty. The horse did its best to avoid her, but the jostling of the crowd forced it to stamp on her foot. A doctor had to be called to bandage her before the wedding procession could get under way.

They were taken through the packed village, with the throng tossing confetti and blossom over them, to the White Horse Inn for the wedding dinner. At the table were thirty-nine people and one dog – Ada, the French bulldog which was Bjorn and Agnetha's pet. The reception represented a *Who's Who* of Swedish musical fraternity. The couple danced to the music of Benny Andersson and the Hep Stars and were serenaded by the Hep Stars lead singer, Svenne Hedlund, who sang 'Sunny Girl'. Even Svenne's wife, Lotta, a black American songstress, sat in on the drums. And Bjorn had to make a contribution. Stikkan Andersson, who wrote a lyric about Bjorn and Agnetha in the few minutes before the wedding ceremony, insisted that the blushing bridegroom stand on the table to sing it. The photographers who had been denied the chance to take pictures in the church took hundreds of shots of the couple at the reception instead. And throughout the reception, a crowd of hundreds of people, ignoring a gentle police request to disperse, stood outside the White Horse chanting: 'We want to see the bride and groom.' It was clear they would not go until they had seen the newly-weds again, so Bjorn and Agnetha walked out on to the balcony at the front of the inn to wave at the crowd. They were rewarded with a cheer that a royal couple would have been proud of. Said Agnetha: 'It was a stirring climax to a wonderful day which I know I will remember every second of my life, even if I live to be a very, very old lady. I was so happy.'

A hammer blow to their happiness arrived the next morning. A telephone call from Stockholm told Bjorn that while they had been celebrating their wedding Bengt Bernhag, Bjorn's discoverer and father figure, had killed himself.

It was a terrible shock, and the gloom could be felt in the hotel. It was particularly terrible for Bjorn, because he and Bengt had been so very close. Bengt had been ill for many years, and after an operation for colitis, had to wear the plastic bag around his middle. Because of this, he could not face going out and meeting people. It made him a sad, lonely, figure. He was so embarrassed by it, he avoided strangers. His life was his family, the studio, and Bjorn's career. Perhaps that was why he was so fond of Bjorn. He focused all his attention on him, and looked on him as a son. When Bjorn had a success, Bengt was so proud, always. He could not bring himself to go to the wedding because he was almost a recluse. He was afraid of people and crowds. And not being able to be with Bjorn on his wedding day was too much for Bengt. He drove off into the forest near Stockholm in his car, taking with him a cushion and a bottle of whisky. He drank all the whisky, then turned the car's engine on. The cushion he put under the exhaust pipe, and lay his head on it in a drunken stupor. He lay down to sleep there and never woke up again. The exhaust fumes killed him.

As soon as Bjorn heard the news, he woke Benny up and the two old friends borrowed a boat to row out into the middle of a nearby lake to discuss it. Putting themselves out of reach of land when they have a particularly knotty problem is a method they have used over the years. They both find that being away from people helps them think better.

Nobody knows what those two discussed out there on the lake. They were out there for hours, talking and talking. When they came back to the inn they were, understandably, silent and brooding. It was a cloud over them, and a shadow on Bjorn's happiness. He was obviously terribly shaken up, but he managed to pull himself together remarkably quickly. When one of the authors spoke to Bjorn later in the day, he could see the cold, clinical man who lived inside him. The sorrow was burning him, but his reaction now was 'Bengt is gone and that's that. I can't do anything about it.' He said that Stikkan had offered to let him and Benny take over as producers with Sweden Music in Bengt's place, and that they had decided to do it. He said: 'It's what Bengt would have wanted us to do. He wouldn't have wanted us to be frozen with unhappiness. It's very tragic, but what can we do now? The work must go on.' A friend said: 'I felt very sad at the passing of Bengt. He had the biggest ears I ever knew for finding the right songs for the right artistes. He was uncanny, and a tremendous hit-maker as a producer. He had that sort of unspoiled ear which allowed him to hear things which other people in the business missed, and he plucked the hits seemingly out of thin air. When he heard the talent in its rawest form, he recognised it and could see the possibilities. He was brilliant, and unerring in his judgement. There was no need for him to see an artiste gilded by the tinsel and trappings. A short tune, a few bars in a cold studio was enough for him. His imagination unfailingly told him the rest.'

At the moment of Bengt Bernhag's death, one of the records he had produced was sitting at the top of the Swedish charts. It was called 'Never More'. The artistes singing it were The Hootenanny Singers.

Normally accounts of suicides are not carried in Sweden because it is considered prying into the grief of tragic people. However, there were reports of Bengt Bernhag's death in the newspapers because of his association with Bjorn and because he took his life on his protégé's wedding day. It was such a poignant story that they could not ignore it.

Bjorn and Agnetha had a sad and thoughtful, and brief, honeymoon. Bjorn said he felt he owed so much to Bengt, who had taught him a hell of a lot about the production side of music. Bengt liked him so much that he passed every secret he knew on to Bjorn, without hesitation. But Bjorn is a resilient young man. He recovered very quickly and has gone on with the business of building his career. He can be very single-minded, and when he is it is an electrifying sight to watch.

After the honeymoon, Bjorn and Agnetha teamed up with Benny again to finish their summer tour of the *folkparks*, where the favourite song in their repertoire was now 'Long Live Love', a fitting wish for the future from the young couple. But Bjorn still seemed to have no inkling of the joint career which lay ahead for himself, his bride, and his friend. He said: 'When we have finished this summer tour, we will go our separate ways as far as showbusiness is concerned. We don't want to be looked on as a sort of sweet, lovey-dovey artiste couple. We both want to be recognised individually, each as an artiste in our own right. That way we won't feel that we are in each other's pockets all the time.'

Agnetha, who had already established her name by her own lights, agreed: 'It's the only way. I don't really want people to point at me and say: "That's Bjorn Ulvaeus's wife." I want to be recognised for my own ability.' It is strange to reflect that they seemed to want to drift apart in the showbusiness sense, rather than weld their partnership even closer.

CHAPTER EIGHT

# ANNI-FRID AND BENNY

Another tour stop. Another motel stop. And a few drinks in the bar, maybe. Benny Andersson grinned as he thought of the people who talked of the wild, non-stop life of showbusiness celebrities. He unpacked and walked down to the bar, ordered a beer, and settled into a chair. He looked around. Just a few people there. Then his eyes settled on a blue-eyed brunette sitting across the room. Very nice. Tall. Willowy. Elegant.

When the barman came around, Benny leaned over to whisper in his ear. 'Who is that girl?' he asked. 'I think I recognise her from somewhere.'

The barman told him: 'She's a singer, too. Anni-Frid Lyngstad. She's good, I hear.'

A few minutes later, Benny walked across to introduce himself. Of course, she knew him. Hep Stars were the big group in Sweden, wowing the kids from Malmo to Lapland. She had a few young men clamouring after her in their minds, too. But all this didn't mean much to the two people sitting in the bar. 'There was nothing electric about our meeting,' Anni-Frid now recalls. 'In fact, it was a bit damp. We had a few beers, a nice chat, and goodbye, that was all.'

Says Benny: 'I didn't feel any rapport between us at all. We just talked about travelling around, a bit about the business, that sort of thing. Nothing special. Nothing very interesting. We had a couple of drinks, I went my way and she went hers. I didn't really expect us to meet up again.'

They did, a short while after, when they were both on a radio quiz show game in Stockholm. This time Benny asked Anni-Frid to dinner, and she accepted. 'I was just at a loose end,' says Benny. 'I thought it would be nice to have a chat.

We did talk, and talk, and talk. For hours and hours. Something happened, we clicked, and suddenly we were enthralled by every word the other had to say. I've never known anything like it. And we haven't stopped talking since.'

Anni-Frid by now had gone through what she calls a 'friendly divorce' from her husband, Ragnar Fredriksson, and was living in a flat in Stockholm. 'It was really a very lonely existence for me,' she says now. 'I think that Benny came along at just the right time. I didn't tell anybody about it, but these were very lonely days for me. I spent a lot of time on my own in the flat, I missed the children a lot, and I began to wonder if it was all worth it. Should I stay to try to really put myself on the map, or should I give it all up, and go to live, if not back with my family, where I could at least be a lot nearer them and see them more often. I think I missed the security of marriage.' Anni-Frid certainly was not very happy about her career at the time. She had recorded nine songs in the previous three years but only two of them had reached the charts, and each for only one week. She was doing some television work, but her material was a trifle old-fashioned, of the 'sentimental ballad' type. She said: 'I've tried pop music, but it's wrong for me. It doesn't fit my style.'

She was right, in that the sort of pop music being offered to her at the time did nothing for her. She had a fine voice, and was really waiting for the right material to come along to do it justice. She had a voice as good as any singer in Sweden at the time, and she felt upset that many other singers with worse voices were doing better than she was, perhaps because of better promotion and that sort of thing. And perhaps because she had not yet found the music which would let the public hear her voice at its best. And at its best, it certainly is fine, warm, and balanced.

On 1 April, 1970, Anni-Frid and Benny moved into a bedsitter flat in the Vasastan area of Stockholm. It was a gloomy, cramped flat on the first floor, in an old house set on a noisy through-traffic street, but it was a true little love nest. However, the cramped conditions presented Benny with a problem. He had nowhere to put his piano. The double bed took up most of the space, leaving only a small amount of room for a sofa, a record player, and a huge pile of records. This, to Benny, was like taking his arms off. He could listen to all the records he liked, but to a musician like him, that is just rubbing in the agony. But even a fanatical musician, given the choice between a piano and a bed, has to choose the bed. There was no way out, there just was not enough room. So he played a lot at the gigs. He didn't mind long shows at all. But, of course, what the audiences didn't realise was that Benny was catching up with his practice onstage; as much as he could. He had to do it somewhere.

Benny recalls: 'Despite this, we were very happy together. But I must admit I became a bit of a music pest whenever I visited a house where they had a piano. I'd be off and playing for hours. I couldn't keep away from it. I'm glad to say that our friends didn't seem to mind. I think they understood my problem. Why, this was probably the first time in my life, or at least since I was a very young boy, that I had lived in a place which did not have a piano which I could indulge myself on.' A church organist who must have known about Benny's deprivation invited him along to play on the church organ. Benny accepted with alacrity, and played in the empty church on the enormous organ for hours and hours. He said: 'I loved it. The organist may have played to heaven, but this was heaven for me.'

Theirs was to be a 'Stockholm marriage', in which the couple lives together without getting the stamp of approval from either the church or the state. Said Benny: 'It's very common in my country. I don't know if it happens more here than anywhere else, or if the truth is that we're a bit more honest and open.' Like so many couples who didn't have the benefit of a wedding anniversary, Benny and Anni-Frid celebrate their 'anniversary' on 1 April each year, studiously ignoring the fact that that date is All Fools Day. 'It's our day, and we celebrate it as happy and vigorously as any churched couple,' said Benny. 'We exchange presents and cards and so on, and perhaps have a celebratory dinner. It's always a happy day, and a very special day for us.'

The couple were officially engaged in August, 1969, at the famous and popular but improbably named 'Hamburger Bors', an elegant restaurant in Stockholm, where Anni-Frid was appearing solo at that time. Engagement time or not, the critics were as brutal as ever with her, pointing out that they considered she was hopelessly stiff on stage, although they and her colleagues had to concede that she had an outstanding voice. The problem seems to have been that she was so shy. She was totally unable to let herself go, and so looked very cold on stage.

Their romance was hailed as pop romance of the year, number two. Anni-Frid was doing long tours with a renowned pianist of the Scandinavian circuit, Charlie Norman. She had, in fact, been on a tour with him when she first met Benny at Malmo. News of their togetherness had got out before the engagement, as is inevitable in the gossip-ridden pop world. At first, Benny had been most reluctant to talk about it, and would only say: 'Yes, we are more than good friends,' which was at least a turn round of the old familiar reply. He told journalists: 'I am in tune with Anni-Frid, but marriage is something we haven't talked about yet.' It is something they have talked about a lot since, and now Benny says: 'If we thought it would improve our relationship, we would get married tomorrow. But as it is, nearly seven years later, we're content to wait. Perhaps we'll get married when we have the time. We're very busy people, you know.' They were both very busy touring in the early days, and so often in entirely different directions. But every opportunity he got, Benny made sure he could get to the town where Anni-Frid was working to spend some time with her. Fellow musicians remember the time when Benny turned up to see Anni-Frid, but in the middle of the day had disappeared. They looked everywhere for him, and were about to give up when they looked into the auditorium where Anni-Frid was to appear that night. Someone was playing on the piano, and there was no mistaking the style and the rhythm. It was Benny, catching up on the practice he was still missing out on. He never missed an opportunity.

A few months after the engagement was announced, *Aftonbladet* newspaper of Stockholm carried a story about Anni-Frid and her break-up with her husband. The article talked about the happiness which was expressed by the pictures she had taken with her husband and two children outside their villa in Eskilstuna. It continued: 'The picture of that happiness was broken when Anni-Frid made an official announcement of her engagement to Benny Andersson of Hep Stars.' It talked of the nasty comments people were making about her break-up and the engagement, repeating the stories that she left her children when she became well-known and went to Stockholm: 'They say she fled from her husband and family in Eskilstuna to work with the big boys.'

Anni-Frid protested: 'Nothing could be more wrong. I kept quiet about it until now because I didn't think it was anyone else's concern. Now I feel that in the face of the stories which I know are circulating I must tell the truth about my separation, my divorce, and my engagement to Benny. The truth is that my divorce was decided about and over long before I met Benny. Ragnar and I met regularly when I went to see the children and we talked on many occasions about our relationship and what we were going to do. Finally, we decided that the best thing for both of us was each to go our own way. It was very carefully thought out, and I know we made the most sensible decision. In fact, Ragnar and I have never been able to talk so easily together and been on such friendly terms as we have since the divorce. I found that amazing, but I've heard that that is the sort of thing that happens with other people, too. I guess we made a mistake by getting married, but we were very young at the time and weren't too clear-headed about what we were doing. So, you see, when I left my family it had nothing, absolutely nothing, to do with Benny. And I shall be so very annoyed if I heard of anybody suggesting that it had.'

Living in the two-bedroom apartment in the centre of Stockholm precluded the possibility of Anni-Frid and Benny having the two children with them. If there was not room to cram a piano in, there certainly was not room for two children –they were then aged seven and three–to run about. Anni-Frid said: 'They live a very happy and good life now. I miss them, but I must not think about missing them. I am happy with my life with Benny and I must be content that they are happy. It would be wrong of me to take them away from a home where so many things are so right for them. I am away so much of the time, and I would not be able to look after them as well as they are cared for now.' But the couple were planning to get a bigger flat, or a house, so that the children could come to live with them on a temporary basis. 'I'd hate to be cut off from the children completely,' she said. 'I hope they'll be able to come to our new place, when we get it, and visit with us from time to time. We both like having them around; they get on well with Benny. Who doesn't?' Later, they moved to a larger flat in the Old Town of Stockholm, set amongst the romantic gabled houses lovingly carved by eighteenth-century stone-masons, and the children were able to visit. 'It means so much to me, to be able to spend some time with them,' said Anni-Frid. 'It's something many people will not understand, but also something that every mother will.'

Anni-Frid and Benny continued their tours, but the strain of being apart told on them from time to time. Once when Charlie Norman, the pianist she worked with, was going up country on a tour, which was taking in some really far flung towns for which they were not being paid very much, Anni-Frid wanted to stay in Stockholm with Benny, who happened to have a few days off. She called up Charlie and suggested that perhaps she could drop out of that part of the tour, and join the troupe later. Charlie told her that if she didn't want to come with them then, she need not bother about the other tours they were doing. She stayed with Benny – and left the Charlie Norman company.

On a personal level, their relationship surprised their

friends. They have always had a very hectic relationship. In fact, it has often been as stormy as the Bjorn and Agnetha match. There was a party at Bjorn's place on Essingen one night when Anni-Frid threw some cups at Benny. He just took it all with a smile and a shrug which, unfortunately, only made Anni-Frid that much madder. But it is very hard to make the easy-going Benny angry. Their personality contrast has always been clearly lined. In a way, it is like a match between a Koala Bear and a Tiger. And, apart from the outbursts from Anni-Frid, there are other vast differences. Anni-Frid is very much the planner, who works things out carefully. In a way she is like Bjorn. Benny, on the other hand, is the opposite to a schemer. He just relaxes, and lets things happen, and does not get uptight with what is going on. Agnetha, oddly, is just like that, and loves her music, like Benny does. So the planners ended up with the easy-going members of the partnership. No doubt that is the best way, for if you get two easy-going people together, the result can be boredom. But if you get two careful planners with a bit of fire in their temperament, the answer can be all-out war.

That tiny flat also presented another problem. Benny loves to listen to classical music like Tchaikovsky and Rossini, and Baroque music. That's not Anni-Frid's bag at all. She goes for jazz music and singing. The flat was so small that it was impossible to hide from the music, and that must have produced a few clashes. But Benny must have had a bit of influence on Anni-Frid's taste in his own gentle way. They go to the opera and ballet when they can find the time.

Anni-Frid has a bit of the iceberg about her character. She is not a cold person, but she certainly is cool. There is also a strange contrast within her which makes her lazy, but also very ambitious. There is no doubt that her career is of paramount importance to her. She had a terrible time when she was in the position of knowing she was a good singer, but saw a lot of less-talented singers being more successful than she was. It did not make her bitter, but it made her that much more determined. She really had to earn her success; for a long time it seemed that she would never make it because she did not have the warmth and personality that makes a popular singer. She was a bit cold for people, and, even if she had an incredibly good voice – she is very clear, very technically correct, and can be strong or soft, in fact she sings just like an instrument – she did not have the right personality on stage to win people over. Benny has helped her get over these problems in his own way. Not by telling her. Benny is the sort of person who shows by example, the only way he knows how. She has mellowed a lot now, although she has that certain aloof air about her, just enough to give her a stage sophistication, but not enough to detach her from the audience. It is so funny to see her and Benny discussing techniques, singing, and music. She takes it all so very seriously, and he makes remarks ranging from light suggestions to outright gags. But what he has given her shows in the very impressive performer she has become.

CHAPTER NINE

# A COUPLE OF ENGAGEDS

Benny and Bjorn were in full flight, continuing their favourite discussion. The piano was closed and Benny, instead of playing, had his arms folded on the lid, and his chin resting on them. He was giving his undivided attention to Bjorn, who had laid his guitar aside to try to put into words what he thought was lacking in them as a team. They had made a couple of records together, and both had disappeared below the surface after making scarcely a ripple. When they appeared on stage, the reception was encouraging enough. But something was certainly missing. This was their favourite discourse. To try to find out what was missing They did not realise that the ingredients which would transform them were only a few feet from them in that flat at that very moment. They were called Agnetha and Anni-Frid, who were sitting in the next room having a chat on a much lighter vein. Bjorn now says: 'It is a constant source of surprise to me that we were together as a foursome, going out together, spending a lot of time together in each other's company, before we realised the natural answer. It wasn't as if Agnetha and Anni-Frid had hidden their abilities as singers. They had become, in their own right, two of the most well-known singers in Sweden. It just took an extraordinarily long time for us to see the possibilities of the chemical reaction which might come about when we were all thrown in together.'

It so happened that Bjorn and Benny had an upcoming engagement to sing at a cabaret restaurant called Valand, in Gothenberg in November, 1970. Bjorn recalled the good reception he, Benny, and Agnetha had received on the *folk-parks* tour. Why not, he reasoned, add Anni-Frid to their act to make up a stage foursome? They called the girls in to pitch the idea to them. The reaction was somewhat short of ecstatic, but they agreed. 'Why not give it a try?' said Anni-Frid.

The restaurant billed them as 'The Engaged Couples', and announced the show as a one-off event. It was a very close facsimile of a disaster. Groups were extremely common in Swedish restaurants at the time and, while the audience quite liked the gentle diversion from their meals, the applause was lukewarm and the performers instantly forgettable. A music critic commented that they were quite pleasant, but that they should not sing together because Agnetha sang out of tune. He said: 'The grouping does not come off.'

The odd thing is that he was right. It was not a good show, and they realised it themselves. He was also right about Agnetha. She does have trouble singing in tune. It does not show so much when she is singing alone, but when she is in a group with the others singing in tune, it does grate on the ears – though she does, in fact, have a very very fine voice. However, they were later able to overcome this problem with re-recording in the studio.

Their other shortcomings were to give them a lot of food for thought. Bjorn recalls: 'There were a whole series of strikes against us from the beginning. For a start, we didn't play our own music, which was probably the biggest mistake. We allowed ourselves to be persuaded against our better judgement because the advice was coming from people we thought knew better than us. They told us: "This is the sort of show you have to present if you are in cabaret. It's the sort of thing that supperclub audiences expect." So we had that type of show written for us, with sweet and happy, and ordinary, cabaret lyrics. That show was in no way like the sort of music we present now. I feel sad when I look back on it now, and I cringe. It was one of the worst times we ever had. We didn't feel anything for the music or the words – and the audience shared our opinion. Fortunately, it did not deter us from singing together, but it made us think a lot about what sort of presentation we should aim for. That sort of night did us a favour in a way. We did just about everything wrong, so by deducing that, we had a pointer to how we should change. The problem, we realised, was in the material and not in us. We came to the conclusion that, whatever we did, we had to make a few changes.'

So the group broke up after one engagement. Each of the four went back to their own tracks. Agnetha was still writing and singing her own songs. One she turned out at her piano, 'If Tears Were Gold', was to be a great success. It was all Bjorn talked about at the time. He told friends 'Agnetha's written a fantastic tune, and I'm sure it will be a hit.' It was another soft and sentimental ballad, which she sang to her own guitar playing. Some time later, it was a solo success for her.

Agnetha made a few appearances as Mary Magdalene in a special staging of 'Jesus Christ Superstar' at Scandinavium, a huge concert hall in Gothenberg. She recorded 'I Don't Know How To Love Him' from the show, and included other songs from it in her repertoire for her *folkparks* tour, which she went off on alone. Anni-Frid had a shot at acting, in a revue at a Stockholm theatre, and followed this up with an LP record of her own. She also sang 'Our Earth Is Wonderful' in the Swedish section of the Eurovision Song Contest, but finished down the list. Benny went on tour with the Hep Stars, and Bjorn rejoined the Hootenanny Singers.

They tried a foursome presentation again in November, 1971, this time at the Tragarn cabaret restaurant in Gothenberg. They still did not click, though the reviewers were a little kinder this time. One said: 'The youngsters give a show with a lot of tempo musically, they have a lot of variations, and sometimes good lyrics. They really go together well on stage.'

But Bjorn's reaction was as before: 'It just wasn't right, and we were going to have to make sure we had one hundred per cent control of the music, the lyrics, the staging, before we could really impose our personality on the presentation.'

Another joint effort was scotched by Stikkan Andersson when Bjorn and Agnetha recorded a duet, appropriately titled: 'This Is The Way Love Starts', which was the story of the two of them. Agnetha made the record on her contract company's label, CBS-Cupol, and Bjorn guested with her. But Stikkan did not like the thought of one of his contract artistes, which Bjorn was, recording for a rival label, so he vetoed a plan to test it on the radio for the hit charts. He was absolutely adamant, even if Agnetha was Bjorn's fiancée.

Agnetha's long-term contract with that record company was to be a continuing problem for all four of them when they did get around to making records together. CBS-Cupol continued to get royalties from Abba successes until 1 January, 1976, when the contract ran out. Until then, Polar Records also had to carry a tagline on the records, declaring that Agnetha was appearing by permission of CBS-Cupol.

Stikkan Andersson had made a promise to both Benny and Bjorn, a promise which he was to regard almost as a holy vow. He said: 'I told them very early on that I was convinced I could give them a big break internationally, as writers and as performers. I explained the very simple figures to them. The population of Sweden is in the region of seven million. But singing to just the English-speaking world would give us an audience of three hundred millions. Their early writing had been in Swedish, but I persuaded them, and they didn't need much pushing, that they should write their lyrics in English. I started helping them with their lyrics, because that part of the business was really my forte, and I knew my guidance would be helpful from there. Our three-way writing partnership has developed very fruitfully from there. They still produce the music, and between the three of us we find suitable matching lyrics. If you say to me that a three-man writing team sounds cumbersome and awkward, I can only agree with you. All I can say is that it works out. And works out very well.' Each had something different to offer. Benny was a pop man, while Bjorn was into nice singing and sentimental music. The Hootenanny Singers produced nice, clean, and easy-going easy-to-listen-to songs, like 'Sweden's Most Beautiful Songs' – one of their best-selling LPs. It was nice, singalong stuff, but musically, it was nothing to write home about. But when these two were tied to Stikkan, the composite result was something totally unexpected. The death of Bengt Bernhag tragically opened to them the chance of expanding their careers into record production, something which both plunged into with relish. Bjorn, with his sharp interest in the technical side of record production, excelled. The duo managed to inject a lot of their own ingenuity and flair into the Polar Records releases. And Bjorn, apart from his own singing and recording, was finding new artistes, and showing himself a true businessman in the Stikkan Andersson mould. But, by vetoing the Agnetha–Bjorn partnership on record, Stikkan was unwittingly slowing down the natural progression to Abba. The normally sure-footed entrepreneur, for once, could not see the magical possibility which was sitting right before his eyes.

An historic milestone which was indelibly to affect their careers came from Bjorn and Benny when they met up with Michael Tretow, the youngest of the technicians at the Metronome Studios in Stockholm. This man was to become the technical genius behind the Abba sound. He worked as a tape technician at Metronome, and took a particular interest in the tapes brought in by the youngsters, with their new beat and sound. This was the early crossroads of pop music, when pop was really getting into its stride. This gave Tretow the opportunity to work with the up-and-coming young musicians in the business; like them he was young, and continually experimenting all the time. He liked the young people, their approach, and their music. It got so that when they took their material to the studios, they would specifically ask that he should handle it. Bjorn and Benny were two of these inventive and bustling musicians. They liked each other's ideas, and they started to work together. Bjorn and Benny worked much longer in the studios than other groups and composers. They built up a good relationship with Michael, experimenting with different approaches to music and sound. That partnership has been building all the time, and it was the link with Tretow which transformed Bjorn and Benny from two very good musicians into a position, with the girls, where they could make what we now know as the Abba sound. There may be a great woman behind every great man, but behind every great group there is a great sound technician. It was Michael Tretow who produced the first LP Bjorn and Benny made together, called 'Lycka' which means 'Happiness'. Not that the record, made in 1970, represented happiness to the two friends. Its impact was negligible.

The path to Abba was paved when Agnetha and Anni-Frid came into the studio to provide backing voices for Bjorn and Benny's recordings. Stikkan Andersson remembers: 'The girls came along strictly to help out their boyfriends. It was nothing more than that. They felt their records needed that something extra, and the voices of the girls, they hoped, would help them along. And it was natural that they should use Agnetha and Anni-Frid for this, rather than bring in other girl singers. Then, one day they came up with some tapes where you could not hear the voices of Bjorn and Benny. Just the girls. They came to me and said: "We don't think we can credit the record to just Bjorn and Benny. The voices are the girls', and they'll have to get recognition for it. We've got to do something, because you can't hear us." Their previous record had been marketed under the name of Bjorn and Benny, with both scoring from their previous publicity with The Hootenanny Singers and Hep Stars. We planned to build them up as a duo, and here they were making incredible suggestions like this. I said: "You are not saying, for heaven's sake, you are not suggesting that we should call you Bjorn, Benny, Agnetha, and Anni-Frid, or something stupid like that, are you?" They said: "That is exactly what we have in mind." I couldn't believe it. I said: "Never. It makes no sense. No sense at all." '

Stikkan pointed out to them that they had not taken the public by storm in their cabaret appearances together, so why should it be any different on the record market? Bjorn and Benny answered, very realistically, that they didn't like the idea of having just their names on a record when it was obvious that the vocals on the record were the voices of two girls. It was an unanswerable case, and Stikkan had to give way. He recalls: 'I had to admit it was silly to call the act Bjorn and Benny when it was obvious the girls were the dominant part of the group. I still didn't like it, but we started calling the act, Bjorn, Benny, Agnetha, and Anni-Frid.'

Their first record together was 'People In Love', with 'Merry Go Round' as the B-side. It went to number two in the Swedish charts, and was a hit in the rest of Scandinavia. Elsewhere, the success was more qualified, but it was a beginning they could build on later. On the American charts, it crawled up to number 115, but that was still the best effort by Swedish artistes till they returned to the American charts as Abba.

Says Benny: 'We were still just four individuals getting together to make some music. But "People In Love" was a song sung and made in exactly the way we wanted. The girls had come into the studio strictly to help out. Nothing more. And out of that relaxed co-operation came this record. I'll never forget the day we played that tape back, and the only voices noticeable were the girls. And those girls together made a tremendous combination sound. It was exactly the vocal sound which has made Abba what it is today. There was a natural fusion which makes it very hard to tell which of them is singing which part of a song. They were just like one voice, and a very beautiful voice at that. It would have been daft to go on with just Bjorn and Benny on the record label.'

Bjorn and Benny bounced from this success – to make another record on their own. 'As you may have gathered, Abba did not just happen overnight,' said Bjorn. Their new record, 'She's My Kind Of Girl', was a hit for the boys, but only in

Japan. 'Which shows you how strange the record business is. There is nothing predictable about it.'

Agnetha and Anni-Frid went back on tour, and the boys got their heads down in the studios. The formula for their future was there, in front of their eyes. They were to pause before they grabbed it.

CHAPTER TEN

# BELLS ARE RINGING

The Eurovision Song Contest, played out before an engrossed Europe-wide television audience of hundreds of millions, has shown itself to be a potential passport to fame over the years. Bjorn, Benny, Agnetha, and Anni-Frid believed that 1973 was going to be their year. The hesitation of the previous couple of years was fading, and they had finally decided that the magical combination of their singing and playing, the lyric writing in harness with Stikkan Andersson, and the technical genius of Michael Tretow was showing them a path to glory ahead.

Bjorn and Benny spent tortuous days composing a piece of music which they found conveyed the unmistakable impression of a bell ringing and ringing. Stikkan provided the words, and the title 'Ring, Ring'.

Said Bjorn: 'It was a simple name and, I suppose, a name which the music was crying out for. Also a title which people anywhere in the world would find easy to say and simple to remember. That's so very important in an international contest of this type. But, of course, a title, brilliant as it may be in its projecting power, is not a scrap of good unless you have the necessary to go with it. We had what it takes in the music. That we were very certain of. Benny and I had worked our hearts out on the melody, in a series of day-long sessions with the piano and guitar. It was a product of our usual method; a matter of spending hour after hour throwing snatches of melody at each other until we built up the whole. Every little detail took us an astonishing amount of time to work out. I remember it took us the best part of a whole day in the studio to work out only how we wanted the bass handled in the musical backing. There was a very special reason for our incredible amount of concentration and perspiration on this melody. We felt that we had a very good chance of winning the Eurovision Song Contest that year. I'm not sure why. It was a confidence born from a feeling that it was going to be our year.

'This inner feeling of confidence was something we all had. We all knew that tingling excitement that anybody on the brink of a breakthrough gets.

'When Benny and I put the final notes of "Ring, Ring" into place, there was absolutely no doubt in our minds that this was the best melody we had ever concocted. All through, we felt that if we kept up our level of concentration and determination, it would be that way. Not that we felt we were sweating and straining at the time. I think it came together so well because we were really enjoying doing it. It felt like a work of art, something which we were going to feel proud of when we looked back on it. I think that feeling got into the melody.'

Stikkan Andersson stepped in to put his mark indelibly on to the song, with lyrics which he felt flowed to fit the mood of the melody. Everything was set shortly before the Swedish heat of the Song Contest, held in February, 1973. But a special drama of their own came along to haunt them on the run in to the heat, which was to be televised from a theatre in the centre of Stockholm. Agnetha was pregnant, and it turned out the baby was due at around the time of the concert.

Said Bjorn: 'We did not know the exact day of the happy event, but it was certain to be within the time. We all did our share of worrying, wondering if the birth would put paid to our chances in the contest. Would the baby arrive before? Or would it wait till after? When I think about the days of waiting beforehand, I can recall all the nerve-racking moments. And the turmoil of the mixed emotions. I was delighted that Agnetha and I were to become parents. But I didn't want that moment to shatter our other dream, of winning the contest. I didn't know what to think, or to pray for.'

The group, under the shrewd direction of Stikkan, prepared a plan of action which would carry them through if they lost Agnetha at the last minute. They lyrics were schemed so that, if necessary, Anni-Frid could take over singing them entirely on her own and cover for her absent friend. Agnetha was photographed in barrel-like condition just before the contest, and everybody was on tenterhooks until the last minute. But Agnetha was confident enough to announce: 'My baby will not arrive until it is all over. I'm sure of that. You don't think it would come along on the day to spoil a moment like this for us, do you?'

The baby did wait, but the group had what turned out to be a far, far more formidable hurdle in the way of victory: a jury of musical experts. Explained Benny: 'I think wiser men than I have said: "Please do not leave our fate to experts." I know exactly what that man meant. But this was in the dark days when the authorities running the Swedish section of the Eurovision Song Contest had this strange notion that the choice of our entry could safely be left to a panel of experts.

'I saw the panel, and it was obvious they would never choose a song which millions of ordinary people would like – the sort of song which we turn out.

'An "expert" is the guy who definitely picks the wrong song. But I suppose that is what experts are for. We see that they have picked something different from the rest of us, and draw a sigh of relief. Only then do we know for absolutely certain that we were, after all, right all the time.

'I'd say that Bjorn, Stikkan, and I were really tuned in to what the public at large was looking for in music. Weren't they the people the contest was supposed to be aiming at? Who were the experts representing, apart from themselves?

'Our track record showed how much we had our finger on the public pulse. Up to that time, we had written about fifty songs together, and something like a third of those had been hits. But those songs had the distinct advantage in that they did not have first to be submitted to a "panel of experts".

Those "experts", I am sure, would have vetoed any of our material which had the necessary vitality and exuberance to be popular. They were about to stamp their seal of disapproval on "Ring, Ring".'

Bjorn, Benny, Agnetha, and Anni-Frid bounced onstage to produce the incandescent fusion of style and feeling which we have come to identify with Abba. The audience roared their approval. They loved them, their zip, their professional cool, and their faultless harmony. There was not a person in the audience who thought they could possibly lose. They were all right in their opinions. Abba should have walked away with it. They were not just head and shoulders above all the other entrants, they were around the corner and out of sight. Not that that was going to have any effect on the panel of experts, sitting there looking like archaic characters in a Victorian workhouse.

The panel of experts lived up to expectations. They gave 'Ring, Ring' the thumbs down, and the group were placed third. How their view differed from that of the average, record-buying public was demonstrated dramatically over the course of the year. 'Ring, Ring' was a number one hit in Sweden, where the panel had rejected it, and, issued as a single and on an LP record of the same name it sold in the hundreds of thousands in Europe.

'Now, wouldn't you say that is pretty good for a failure?' said Bjorn. 'It was a tremendous disappointment to us not to go on to the finals, because we really felt we had a first class chance of taking the first prize. But, as the months went by, and time eased our wretched feeling of let-down, we began to look at it in quite another and more philosophical way. If anybody at the time had told me it was a blessing in disguise, I would have had to repeat the famous phrase of Winston Churchill and say, "In that case, it must be very well disguised." However, that was precisely how we did come to look on it. Stikkan had seen that we could project ourselves on to the world stage through a successful appearance in the contest, and because we lost, precisely because we lost, he was granted a year in which he could lay the very careful preparations for 1974, which *was* going to be our year. He has always had unlimited faith in us, and this was undimmed by the careless rejection at the hands of that panel. As far as he was concerned, it was inevitable that we were going to win, and he put all his incredible amount of energy into preparing the market for us, so that at exactly the right moment – when we carried off the Eurovision trophy – he could strike.'

Agnetha's baby – which turned out to be a girl, whom they called Linda – made her appearance four days after the contest, at a hospital in Stockholm, less than a couple of miles from the concert hall which was the scene of their defeat. Bjorn was with Agnetha all the time, to hold her hand during the actual moment of birth. 'I think this is a moment that every husband should share with his wife,' he said. 'I know a lot of people are squeamish about it, but I feel I really shared the birth with Agnetha.'

When Linda was four days old, she gave her first press conference, lying in her mother's arms on the hospital bed while photographers dressed in germ-restricting white smocks and face masks crowded around. Linda did not make a sound, but Bjorn proudly announced: 'Our house is full of toys. I've been buying them for months. It's been a bit difficult not knowing whether we were going to have a girl or a boy. I wonder if she'll like train sets? I am taking my fatherhood very seriously. I have read a lot of books telling all about young children, so I think perhaps I will be some help.'

The hospital press conference had Bjorn written all over it. He is as sharp as a tack, and a business brain as finely tuned as his was not going to pass over the chance of getting what turned out to be some very original and very loud publicity for the group. And why shouldn't he? As he explained, it did the baby no harm at all, and the photographs that were taken then will be something for her to treasure into her old age. How many babies gave a press conference when they were just a few days old?

Agnetha was vibrant with happiness. It was the proudest

moment in her life, and she has had a few proud highspots. But none has meant as much to her as Linda. She has continued to be a one-hundred-per-cent member of the group, very much an indispensable part, but from that moment, the most important thing in her life has been her marriage and Linda. If showbusiness closed its doors to her, she would not bat an eyelid, but would retreat comfortably and happily to the role of housewife and mother, and thoroughly enjoy devoting all her time to looking after her daughter. She is quite besotted with her, and misses her every second they are away on tours.

She has stopped writing songs, because the sort of material she wrote was just what the group were not looking for. It would be totally unsuitable for them. And after 'Ring, Ring', there was no question about the future of these four artistes. They had welded together as a group with a very special joint talent, and that is how they were going to stay.

The fact that 'Ring, Ring' did so well, even without winning the contest, was a confirming sign to Stikkan Andersson that his judgement had been right. He said: 'It showed that we were definitely on the right track, that our type of music was what people wanted to hear. I knew that if we held true to our musical convictions, we were going places. The Eurovision Song Contest I still saw as a great launching pad for us, but I knew that even without it, we could make it.'

Another single, 'Love Ain't Easy', was issued that year. Once again, it carried all their names as the artistes. But every time anyone referred to the group, which was still without a name, they had to contend with the unwieldy mouthful of 'Bjorn, Benny, Agnetha, and Anni-Frid'. Said Stikkan: 'Something had to be done about it, obviously. In private, in fact, a memo form of the name had been devised, picking out the initials of the first names to produce A–B–B–A. If I spoke to a journalist, or a promoter, or a musician, I would refer to them as Abba. So, for some time before we officially launched the name, Abba was being used behind the scenes. Disc jockeys picked it up, and they used the shorthand form to describe the group, rather than saying all their names.

'By now, it had become obvious to me as well that the girls were as important as Bjorn and Benny in the group. I had to start including them in everything, but saying all the names each time became very tiresome, so Abba was the name which got into common usage in the business, and slowly the name spread. It was quicker and easier, and Abba became used more and more. It reached the stage where the name was theirs long before they officially adopted it.'

A Swedish newspaper, *Goteborgs–Tidningen*, the Gothenberg daily, stepped in to help. They asked their readers to vote for a name for the group. A newspaper executive explained: 'Here was a group of fine young Swedish musicians and singers who were clearly on their way to putting Swedish music on the map, and were going to be fine ambassadors for Sweden – and there was no name for them. We decided we would give them a hand, and see if our readers could find a name which the group could wear proudly.' The suggestions for names flowed in. Some were good, some bad, many mediocre. Flower Power was quite popular. Other offerings were: Black Devils, Golden Diamonds, Baba. Thankfully eighty per-cent of those who wrote in, opted for Abba. So Abba they became.

Said Stikkan: 'Their choice was probably helped along because disc jockeys had already adopted the name. But in the face of an eighty per-cent vote, who were we to refuse? And, as you have already guessed, it fulfilled the most important requirement of all. *We* liked it. It's catchy, brief, easy to remember in any language. It came from the chance that their combined initials made it, and that was just a nice, pleasant coincidence that we were very happy to grab and make capital out of. I told Bjorn, Benny, Agnetha, and Anni-Frid: "Abba is a name that will be on the lips of people all over the world." I'm very glad to say that before much time had passed my prediction turned out to be right.'

There was, however, one small impediment in the way of

their adoption of the name. Though people round the world look on it as an absolute original, in Sweden they knew it was not. The name was already in use, and could be seen at just about any delicatessen or supermarket in the country on any day. 'Abba' is the name of an enormous Swedish factory which smokes herrings by the million.

Said Stikkan: 'There was a lot of laughs going around, and a few jokes that I won't care to repeat. It was a big joke that, apparently, we were named after a herring factory. That was not the case at all. We had come up with the name independently; we certainly did not steal it from the factory. Before we took up the name, I took care to call the Abba company first and ask them if they had any objections to us using the name. They told me they did not mind at all, and I was very relieved to hear that. Because, by that time, we had been unofficially dubbed Abba by so many people that we'd have been very hard put to find a name which had anything like the same impact.

'As it turned out, it has been a very happy relationship between us and the other Abba. They have been pleased that every time we appear and our name is used, we advertise their herrings. And millions of shoppers are reminded every day about us when they walk by the fish counter in shops all over the country.'

Anders Ekstrom, boss of the other Abba concern in Stockholm, chuckled about the connection. He said: 'When the group first appeared using the name Abba, we were asked if we had a financial involvement in them. I assured everybody that was not true. But we are pleased to be associated in any way with four such fine young people.'

When the group went on to win the next Eurovision Song Contest in Brighton, Ekstrom said: 'You can count us as happy as all other Swedes that Abba won. Perhaps even a little bit happier than most, because they are giving indirect publicity to our products.' The Abba concern was so elated by that success, that they looked into the possibility of launching an advertising campaign in the wake of the group's victory.

Unfortunately, they had to drop the plan because they had done nothing in advance to prepare for it. Like most other people in Sweden, they had not believed in Abba's chances of winning. Said Stikkan: 'I had confidently predicted that we were going there to take the trophy, but there were too many faint hearts, who did not share my confidence.'

However, a thinly veiled warning about the group's use of the name was to come shortly afterwards. The company's personnel manager, Per Brolund, said: 'We have gained more by our associating with the group than anything else. Because of them, our name is publicised in places we would never have dreamed of. But a word of caution for the future. We would not be happy about their use of the name if they were to, perhaps, give it a bad reputation by some untoward public behaviour or something of that kind. We have the Abba name protected as our copyright for food. We didn't think we'd have to protect the name in relation to pop groups.'

CHAPTER ELEVEN

# BRIGHTON VICTORY

Perhaps it was the defeat of 'Ring, Ring' which unconsciously inspired Abba's choice of song for their entry into the 1974 Eurovision Song Contest fray. 'Waterloo' was its title. It is a word which has found a place in the English language as a symbol of defeat. What schoolkid has not heard the phrase, 'He met his Waterloo', to describe someone losing in a challenge in life. Abba were to transform Waterloo, the name of an obscure village in Belgium where the French Emperor Napoleon lost his empire, into a talisman of victory. It was to mark the foundation of their world-conquering empire.

Their march on Brighton to capture the title was organised with military precision, a precision bearing all the hallmarks of a general of genius and cunning – Stikkan Andersson. It was Stikkan who devoted weeks to organising a world-wide review of music trends, collecting intelligence reports from a network of contacts, who felt the pulse of the music public. The object? To establish just what the judges of the contest would be looking for, and try to fathom what was most likely to appeal to them.

Stikkan's office was like the campaign room of a conquering general. His reports from 'intelligence agents' all over the world were scattered on his desk. Seated around him, assessing the reports, were his 'chiefs of staff', the members of Abba. There was an electric feeling about them at this time. Visitors felt the confidence they were projecting. They were experienced campaigners by now, and they were brimful of confidence, so much more so than even in the previous year. They were fighting fit, and pawing at the ground, eager to get to grips with the enemy.

The intelligence reports told them that the laurels that year would fall to an upbeat pop tune. Common sense told Stikkan that the title would have to be one which was as pronounceable and recognisable to Bulgarians and Japanese as it was to English or French audiences. Said Stikkan: 'With this preliminary research over, we then had to find a song and melody which fitted all the requirements. That was the moment the hard work started.' They had an impressive store of melodies in an unfinished state, one of which was going to be their ammunition. Stikkan, Bjorn, and Benny spent hundreds of hours on this quest, looking for the tune which fired all their instincts. Finally, they selected one with a particularly fetching staccato boom-boom flavour to it, a demonstrative upbeat pop tune. 'It was exactly what we were searching for,' said Stikkan. 'Now all we had to do was match the lyric – and the title.' The title came first. Stikkan and the boys scoured reference books for a one word title which would launch itself at listeners in any part of the globe. A history book turned out to be its hiding place, and the title was 'Waterloo'.

Said Bjorn: 'I'm sure this has the sound of a cold, computer-like approach to something which is essentially artistic. But you must also agree that the song we produced did not convey that at all. We couldn't just adopt a hit-or-miss attitude to something like this. Another miss in the contest might have got us the reputation of the also-rans. We didn't want that. There was only one place we wanted to find ourselves. At the top.' All three made their contributions to the lyric – and that history book was to stay with them as part of the team. Though in the loosest sense. Napoleon did not surrender at Waterloo, as the words of the Abba song claim. 'Don't take it too seriously,' said Bjorn. 'After all, we were only borrowing from history. We were not trying to put a history lesson together.'

Next step in Stikkan's orchestration of their road to victory was a visual presentation which would ensure that, for the millions of television viewers, Abba would be an enduring memory. Their musical director – whose chore was to conduct the accompanying musicians – was persuaded to lay aside his black tie and tails to don what must rate as the most distinctive and unusual outfit in the history of the baton waving brigade: a dress uniform of an Imperial soldier of Napoleon's army, complete with the famous sideways-sitting black hat. 'He did not mind at all,' said Stikkan. 'And his impact was tremendous – and unforgettable. An incredible number of people were to comment on his appearance, and how it matched our song.' The four members of the group were not to be put in the shade. The glitter of their sartorial presentation was to overshadow even the Gallic elegance of their conductor. Inspired by a star-spangled performer from the home country of pop, England, their clothes were of silks of many colours, festooned with sequins. They outglittered Gary Glitter, their inspiration.

Shoulder to shoulder, Abba strode into the front line to face up to their first challenge of the campaign, a local skirmish in Stockholm, in the form of the Swedish heat of the contest. This time the concert hall ordeal was to be their ally instead of the enemy. The controversial panel of experts of the previous years had been thrown out, in favour of a 'people's jury', consisting of three hundred men and women, chosen statistically from the everyday folk of Sweden.

'This made so much more sense than the old arrangement, which was so silly, because it, surely, could only produce a victor which would get the thumbs down from the non-expert jury of the final,' said Benny. 'This time, we were being listened to by ordinary folk, the people who appreciated our music. They were not to disappoint us. We could tell by our reception from them that things were going to be different this year.'

They were. Abba won by a knockout, and turned to face the more formidable challenge presented by the sixteen other entrants, in a friendly twentieth-century battle for European domination, a combat which Napoleon, peering through the mists of time, surely would not have believed possible.

Stikkan stood at the helm, determined to put in a challenge which the more favoured musical giants of Europe would find unanswerable. It was something like the tiny ships of Drake facing the majestic powers of the Spanish Armada. The odds looked insurmountable; where was the Swedish tradition which showed they could topple their acknowledged musical masters? Anybody who suggested Sweden had a real chance was looked at as if he were crazy. To most people, the thought of Sweden finishing in the number one slot was about as likely as Albania carrying off the World Cup in soccer. But Abba had a remarkable and confident captain in Stikkan Andersson. He said: 'I was convinced we were going to win in Brighton, the venue chosen as the location for the final that year. For the first time, we dropped the individual names of the group and billed them just as "Abba". We'd already made sure there was going to be no identity problem with the title. With that going for us, it would not have made much sense to complicate matters by using all their names. Not when we had a zinger of a name like Abba to use. We didn't want people hearing the names Bjorn, Benny, Agnetha, and Anni-Frid read out and asking: "Who the hell are they?" Abba was one of our master cards, and we were to make sure it was dealt properly.'

There was no question of Stikkan Andersson and his organisation cooling their heels while they waited the few weeks for the march on Brighton. Stikkan still had a lot of preparation work to do. He saw to it that 'Waterloo' was sold to every country in Western Europe, and it moved into the charts in some countries even before the final was held. He also spent 50,000 Swedish kroner on a PR splurge, preparing packs of biographies and photographs, to mount a campaign to coincide with the win he was sure they were heading for.

Explained Stikkan: 'Even if we slipped at the last hurdle and did not win, it was not going to be a waste for us. This preliminary work virtually ensured that, come what may, "Waterloo" was going to become an international hit. Remember that "Ring, Ring" did very well in many parts of Europe as well as in Sweden, even though we failed to win in Stockholm with it the year before. That was a clear and unmistakable signal to me that, even without a win in the Eurovision Song

Contest, we could break out into the open and exciting country of the world market. It was only the beginning, but a firm start which we were going to build on. We were not scared of the tradition, which said that Swedish groups were all right for Scandinavia, but had no chance when it came to matching them against outsiders. This tradition asserted that the only groups worth a candle came from Britain or America. The reaction of people when you spoke about a group from here was: "Swedish? You must be joking." I have never held with traditions of that type. The taboo against Swedish groups could be laid, and we were the people to do it. When we won in Stockholm – thank heaven for the ordinary folk, who like our music – we really started to flex our muscles. I could feel my faith in our chances transferring to the four members of the group. They were starting to get that same feeling that this was it.

'A lot of talk has gone on about our selection of the name "Waterloo", the symbol of Napoleon's defeat. Some people asked me: "Aren't you afraid that it will be a jinx for you, that it may take you to defeat, as well?" My answer was: "Forget about what it means. We are talking about a song, and about music. And, anyway, I'm not superstitious."

'The money we put into the promotional budget was in no way a gamble. I was preparing the ground, something which had to be done, and that preparation was to be rewarded when I saw "Waterloo" in the charts all over Europe.'

The logistics of Stikkan's drive were impressive. Even before Brighton, 110,000 singles and 97,000 long players of 'Waterloo' were sold in Sweden; it was released in twelve countries; and, apart from Sweden, the song had appeared in the charts in Denmark and Norway. He had made sure it was the first song from the finals to be released, and the dividends were instantaneous.

If Stikkan was not superstitious, the members of Abba were, and unashamedly so. Anni-Frid appeared everywhere, wearing a wide-brimmed sombrero. She joked to the press: 'I never take it off, because it hides the fact that I haven't had time to wash my hair.'

In fact, it had become the good luck talisman for Abba. Benny confided: 'It's our good luck hat. I know a lot of people might laugh at that, but ours is a business full of such superstitions, and we're not immune from such things. Once it had become something of a good luck charm to us, it had to stay. If she had put it aside, there would have been a howl of protest from the rest of us. There were stories that she even slept in it, but I can tell you that was not true. Can you imagine how uncomfortable that would have been? But it was certainly a mascot, and one I was glad to see staying with us right to the end. She doesn't wear it very much now, but it does have a pride of place in our home. It's the least it deserved, after accompanying us all that way.'

Another talisman for the group was Bjorn's secret weapon, a guitar which had been designed to look like a five pointed star; it matched the sparkle of the rest of their presentation perfectly. For the five hundred million plus viewers who watched the final on television in their homes around Europe, the memory of that guitar was to be indelibly etched on their minds. It was all part of the Abba philosophy which imprinted itself on the world of pop: Just try to forget us!

Right up to the moment of the final in Brighton, they were the unknowns, the classic 'dark horse' in the race. At a cocktail party held just a few days before, Swedish journalists were always being asked: 'Who are they? What do they do? Where did they come from?' Anni-Frid was the one who really impressed, and it was her cool aloofness which did it for her. Her answers were always careful and well-considered. With nods of approval, the journalists would ask: 'Who is that Abba girl? She appears so well-educated, which is unusual in these circles.' That's the Anni-Frid effect. She wasn't particularly well educated, but her bearing and poised presentation and her incisive talk all give the impression of a lady who was. She does not try to give that impression, it just comes very naturally to her.

Bjorn, Benny, Anni-Frid, and Agnetha, who had been launched officially as Abba only a couple of months earlier, travelled to Brighton a few days before the contest, to enable them to set up their music and presentation, rehearsals, and a bit of acclimatisation. A third good luck charm travelled with them, tucked into Agnetha's baggage. It was a stuffed donkey, which some enthusiastic Swedish fans had presented to Agnetha a few months earlier. She said: 'He's a great character, even if he is quite large. I kept him with me while we sailed through the Swedish final, and I felt that he was going to bring us luck, so he came on the journey to Brighton with us. The others had a bit of a laugh when I told them I was bringing the donkey. But I insisted he was my mascot and would bring us good fortune. What's wrong with having a good luck mascot? And, you know, I think he did bring us luck.'

Benny remembers the flight over vividly. 'When we travel, we're normally chatting away happily to each other, making jokes and so on. It's a really relaxed feeling that we manage to generate. Well, on this flight, only a few words passed between us. I think the tension of it all, and the realisation that we were finally on our way to something we had dreamed of for so long got through to us. I looked at the faces of the others, and I saw just the kind of tension that I felt in my stomach. We didn't talk about it, but it was there, sort of hanging over us, and we tried to ignore it, hoping it would go away. I'm glad to say it did, and the relaxation I felt strolling around Brighton, breathing all that beautiful, fresh, spring air was something fantastic. The town had a fascinating look, and is like I always dreamed a British coastal town should look. I've promised myself that one day I'll spend some time there and get to know the place really well. The bracing sea air seemed to affect the others in the same way, and we were our old selves in no time at all. That is, until we were about to step onstage to present "Waterloo" to five hundred million people. Then all the knots came back again.'

For Brighton, the contest, to be held in the concrete-and-glass splendour of The Dome, a newly-built 'entertainment

KEYSTONE/SVENSKT PRESSFOTO

Abba . . . (left to right) Annifrid, Benny, Agnetha and Bjorn.

REX FEATURES

Abba promoting Arrival.

KEYSTONE/SVENSKT PRESSFOTO

Beautiful girls, beautiful music.

INTERNATIONAL MAGAZINE SERVICE

Benny Andersson's former fiance Christina Gronvall, with their two children Peter and Helena.

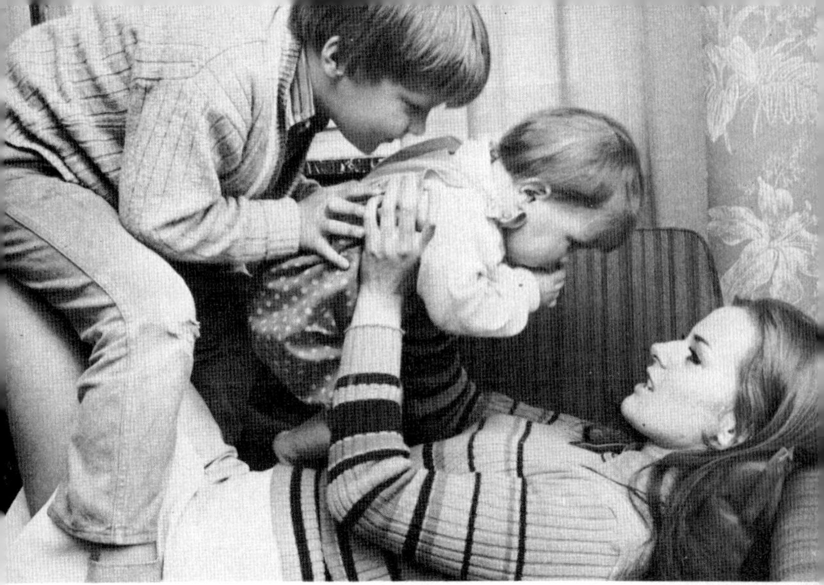

BO DENNEMO

Annifrid's two children from her former husband, Hans and Lise-Lotte.

Annifrid with Benny.

PRESS ASSOCIATION/PRESSENS BILD

PRESS ASSOCIATION/PRESSENS BILD

Agnetha and Bjorn on their wedding day.

Agnetha with her baby Linda.

PRESS ASSOCIATION/PRESSENS BILD

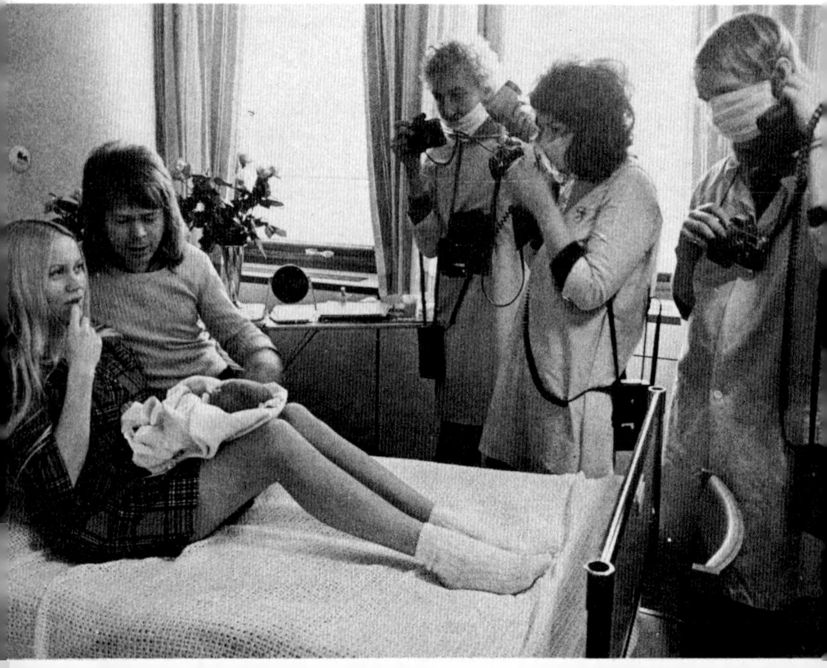

PRESS ASSOCIATION/PRESSENS BILD

At home with Linda.

KEYSTONE

Moment of triumph: the group after their victory in the Eurovision Song Contest.

KEYSTONE

SYNDICATION INTERNATIONAL

Abba in London, February 1978.

PRESS ASSOCIATION/PRESSENS BILD

Benny and Bjorn, the two songwriters.

CAMERA PRESS

In typical stage-gear.

PRESS ASSOCIATION/PRESSENS BILD

The fifth member of the group . . . Stig Andersson, the manager.

Relaxing on their hideaway island. SYNDICATION

KEYSTONE/SVENSKT PRESSFOTO

Appearing on a TV show.

In Warsaw with some of their record awards.

PRESS ASSOCIATION/PRESSENS BILD

CAMERA PRESS

On the streets of Stockholm.

Their happiest days are spent on the island.

PRESS ASSOCIATION/PRESSENS BILD

PRESS ASSOCIATION/PRESSENS BILD

On the move again.

complex', was giving it its biggest moment since the days of the old London-to-Brighton veteran car rallies. Posters on walls and buses proclaimed 'Brighton welcomes Eurovision.' The hotels were packed with musicians and pop journalists from every part of Europe. And the cameras and cables of the television crews looked as if they were going to take over the town. The town's tradesmen were happy, business was booming as it had in no April within living memory, and council officials reckoned Brighton was getting a million pounds worth of publicity.

Stikkan Andersson arrived with Abba, but did a smart about turn to London, where he played the group's tape of 'Waterloo' to a music publisher. Said Stikkan: 'I would not dream of embarrassing that man by telling you his name, but he rejected the opportunity out of hand. He listened to it very politely, then told me in so many words that I was an idiot if I thought that record could ever be successful. He singled out the electric piano sound and said: "It's impossible with that on the record. You must get an up-to-date approach. This is so old hat. The kids will never go for it." He didn't think the tape had anything. I would have come away from there depressed if I had not been so confident that I had a hit on my hands. It amazes me that he particularly did not like the sweeping piano sound, which I believe is so much a part of the Abba success story. He was most embarrassed a few days later, but I did not want to rub salt in the wound. I didn't mention our meeting. What would I gain by dancing openly on his bad judgement? He must have felt bad enough about it already, without me adding to his problems.'

He went straight back to Brighton, where he found the bookmakers' judgement was as far out as that music publisher's. Abba, which had started out among the favourites at 6–1, had slipped to 20–1. Stikkan immediately bet twenty pounds on an Abba win, and Benny followed him in with a ten pounds bet. Said Stikkan: 'I could not believe the odds. I didn't expect us to be the favourites, but this was ridiculous. And something much too good to miss. As far as I was concerned, it was like them giving me the money. That's how confident I was.' Favourite at this stage was the English singer, Olivia Newton-John, whose entry, 'Long Live Love', was quoted at 5–1. Close on her heels were the Dutch duo, with the unbelievable name of Mouth and McNeal, who were 6–1. 'I could not understand the odds, it seemed incredible,' said Stikkan. 'But I was looking at the contest from a different standpoint to the bookmakers. I suppose I should have felt sorry for them, but it is extremely hard to feel sorry for bookmakers, isn't it?'

Nervous police chiefs made Brighton an extremely security-conscious town. Everybody who went into The Dome had to have special security passes, and were still made to walk through a metal-detector doorway. Top of the security risks were the contingents from Israel, Greece, and Ireland. The danger to them was considered so great, that they were herded together into their own heavily-guarded floor at a hotel. Policemen were on constant patrol on the floor, and all the doors and corridors were carefully watched. The security clampdown, which was brought in because of the IRA bombing campaign then raging in England, is Anni-Frid's most vivid memory of her time in Brighton. She recalls: 'It seemed that I could not move anywhere without someone wanting to stop and search me, go through my handbag, and so on. I didn't mind it at all, because any international gathering seems to be considered fair game by the terrorists who are plaguing the world. It was a sober reminder to us that, peaceful as that beautiful town may look, just below the surface, danger could be waiting for any one of us without a moment of warning.'

Rehearsals were held on the day before the final, and Abba ran into an unexpected hitch which threatened their chances. They had brought with them from Sweden a 'Waterloo' background tape, with music they had recorded in their own studios in Stockholm. But when they played it through their loudspeakers in The Dome, they realised it did not sound right.

Benny recalls: 'It was a very hairy moment. It sounded so weak when we played it through the loudspeakers, yet it had been perfectly all right, or seemed to be, before we left Stockholm. We were all worried about it, and crowded around the engineer, looking like the four worried men. The problem was that "Waterloo" is a tune which must boom out, or its best effect is lost. The engineer tinkered about with the equipment for what seemed ages, then told us that he was sure he could sort out the problem. We hoped he was right. It was a long way to come to be let down by some equipment. It would have been a heart breaker.'

Abba and the sixteen other contestants – there should have been seventeen others, but France dropped out as a mark of respect to President Pompidou, whose death had just been announced – went through their rehearsals. Said Bjorn: 'We had settled down well by now, and we gave a performance in that rehearsal which I think we would have been pleased with in the contest. But that sound was going to give us a few more anxious moments.'

It was Agnetha's 24th birthday that day and, after the rehearsal, they went back to their hotel, where they cracked a bottle of champagne. 'That helped to relax us even more,' said Agnetha. 'With the last hours before the final ticking away, our tension was climbing to a peak again. I think it has to do that if you are going to give your best performance. If you feel too free and easy, that can come through in a show. But if you are tensed up and the adrenalin is flowing, that drives you on to your maximum effort. And that is what we were aiming at the next day, after all. A few niggling doubts about that tape were still around, but, to use the old show business expression, we hoped it would be all right on the day. We did try not to talk about the upcoming final, but we all knew that just below the surface, we, naturally, all had it filling our minds. Despite that, we all managed to get off to bed early and fall into a fantastic ten hours' sleep. I don't know how we managed that. Perhaps it was sheer nervous exhaustion.'

Saturday, 6 April, was the day of the final. Benny was first into the breakfast room, but found he could not eat his breakfast. 'I told myself that skipping breakfast was not uncommon for me, so not to worry about it,' he said. 'I just sat there, looking out at the sea and the promenade. But I think the tension was even getting through to me. Well, it was a big moment in our lives that day. One slip, and we'd have wasted all our efforts that had brought us this far. I saw some of the other contestants ploughing their way through enormous breakfasts, and I wondered how they did it. Some bacon sounded a great idea, but I knew I could not manage it.'

The sound engineer came along to brighten their day immediately by announcing that he had resolved the problem with the tape and they spent the rest of the morning preparing for the 2 p.m. dress rehearsal.

'I could feel the tension building up all the day,' said Bjorn. 'We were greatly relieved when we got the news from the engineer, but as we went ahead with our preparations, there was no avoiding that tingling feeling in my stomach. We put on our colourful clothes, and with all those sequins, we really sparkled. We looked splendid I thought, and I remember saying a little wish that our performance would sound as good as we looked. If that happened, I figured, all these other poor people here don't have a chance. The tape was played – and it sounded fantastic. I suppose it was a reaction to hearing it in its weakened state, but its boom-boom effect seemed to be magnified. It was even more powerful than I remembered it. It was just the sort of boost our wavering spirits needed at that moment.

'We bounced through the dress rehearsal in fine style. I felt we were like a boxing contender who had reached peak fitness at exactly the right moment. Mind you, we were still tense under it all. I knew I was, and I could feel that the others were. Benny was all smiles, as usual, but there was something there. And the girls, who are always carrying that cool look, never betray nerves to anyone in the audience. With me, it was different. There was nothing on the surface, but I could feel there was an underlying tension.'

A Brutus-like stab in the back came that day to hound their confidence. Swedish pop writer Christa Lundblad of *Dagens Nyheter*, Sweden's biggest morning paper, launched an abrasive and insensitively-timed attack on 'Waterloo'. He wrote: 'The start has been borrowed from the English group 10cc; the refrain is very similar to "Build Me Up Buttercup", which was a 1968 hit for the English band Foundations; and the saxophone playing is taken from early soul music, like the Junior Walker tunes. But the oldest contribution is from the First Piano Concerto of Tchaikovksy, the Russian composer. This Concerto has been played a lot over the years, and they must have heard it a lot before they wrote "Waterloo".'

This might have shaken a group which was less closely knit. Benny said: 'Sure, I've listened to the music that was mentioned, and I love classical music. But to say "Waterloo" was put together with bits stolen from here and there is a shocking nonsense. Fortunately, it didn't worry us at all, because we knew that what we had put together was something entirely our own, and something that was completely original in concept.'

Still, it was a nasty blast, and totally unjustified. Here was a group who were presenting something entirely different and original, and they were getting hammered as copy-cats. It was just this very originality which had taken Abba to where they were. This attitude has been very common among Swedish critics: like the others, Lundblad was totally unable to believe that Swedish musicians could produce anything worthwhile and original. In a way, the critics haven't changed even now. They still can't believe in the Abba miracle.

After the dress rehearsal, Benny and Anni-Frid went off to a restaurant, while Bjorn and Agnetha went to one in another part of town. Said Bjorn: 'We spend enough time with each other to be able to say, "Okay, we'll split for a meal." After all, we don't want to be in each other's pockets all the time. We all understand that, and, though we get on tremendously well all together, we know there is a limit. I took Agnetha for a walk afterwards and we didn't meet up with the others till we went back to The Dome that evening.'

At The Dome, the excitement in the audience was riding high. Backstage, where all the artistes were packed into one room, the tension was reaching an unbearable level.

Said Benny: 'I wondered how they managed to get so many people in that room. It was jammed. And you could see everybody looking at each other, sort of weighing up the opposition, I suppose. I allowed myself just one beer, which tasted so good. Then it was just a matter of sitting around, waiting for our turn to go on. I've read about people waiting for minutes which seemed like hours to pass. That night I knew exactly what they meant.

'We had to get out of that room. In there, you could cut the atmosphere with a knife. And all those nervous faces looking at each other. It was too much. So we went out and along a corridor to the musicians' dressing room. The people from Yugoslavia were already there – they must have wanted to spend a bit of time away from the nervous crowd, too. We settled down in chairs to watch the show on a monitor set in the room.

'I think all of us in the contest would really have liked to go first. Then your song is finished and out of the way, and you can have the pleasure of watching everybody else sweat. Anyway, the draw had as at number eight, right in the middle, and we watched the first seven songs on the television. I suppose we could have watched them onstage, but watching the television made us feel that bit more detached, and we wanted to see their effect on the small screen. One by one they went, and as they came back offstage, we could see how nervous they were. And you can imagine how dry our mouths were, sitting there and waiting. I felt sorriest for those who had to wait right to the end. Their tension must have been unbearable.

'In dream-like movements, we heard ourselves called, and we walked along the hallway into the cauldron of the theatre.

The tingling had turned to numbness, and suddenly we were on stage. All I could think about was the five hundred million people watching. Then strange thoughts started rushing around my head. I kept thinking that something terrible was going to happen. That we were going to forget the words in front of all those people.

'The four of us were snatching glances at each other. I think in a situation like that, it's a great help, a comfort, to have four of you out there. You sort of draw a bit of strength from the others, and they draw some strength from you. If I had been up there on my own, I think my nervousness would have been magnified fourfold. We belted through "Waterloo", and it sounded to us that it went well. Our nerves disappeared as the first notes struck up, and we got into our stride. By the time we were through the first line, "My, my, at Waterloo Napoleon did surrender", the tension was a bit of history itself. We were too busy playing and singing to remember to be on edge. Our musical director looked a remarkable sight in his imperial uniform; a bit funny, really, and I think that little snatch of humour helped us. Then it was all over, and we were back in that tiny room, crammed in with all the other artistes who were waiting to hear their fate.'

Anni-Frid recalls: 'The wait for the votes to be counted was absolutely unbearable. Everybody – including us – was so excited that it hurt. I'm convinced the tension we all felt pushed the temperature of that room up. Now we had been onstage, I could feel the nervousness draining out of me. I felt as if I was deflating like a balloon. I could see exactly the same thing was happening to the others. But for the poor souls who were still waiting to go on, the strain was multiplying and multiplying.'

The press representatives gathered had not confided their opinions to Abba, but from rehearsal time on they had been sure the group was going to win. Their memorable presentation in glittering colour, helped by the musical director, who looked something like a refugee from a Gilbert and Sullivan light opera, had ensured the memory of Abba was going to be etched on millions of minds. Richard Last, a television writer for the London *Daily Telegraph*, was to record: 'Looking like silver-booted visitants from a more carefree planet, they shook Brighton's sedate Dome with an ear-and-eye catching number that began: "At Waterloo Napoleon did surrender, oh, yeah." '

When the last of the contestants had been onstage, they all jammed into the small room, which was now packed to bursting point. 'I would not have believed it possible to get so many people into that room, unless I had seen it myself,' said Benny. 'For me, my head was still buzzing, and I could feel my heart pounding. None of us in that room made a sound as we stood, our eyes riveted to the tiny monitor screen as the votes came in from the various countries. The voting went to and fro, and I remember one time when I thought our chance of winning was drifting away, and I felt so disappointed. I took my coat off and sat down in a chair. Then Finland gave us five points, and put us into the lead. I snatched up my coat and put it back on, and stood their watching the screen, not blinking.'

The atmosphere increased as the count rolled slowly in. Benny, Bjorn, Agnetha and Anni-Frid found themselves jammed together near the door and, at Bjorn's suggestion, they slipped out of the door and into the musicians' room to try to get away from the atmosphere. But an officious security man spotted them and explained carefully that the security rules covering the contest said clearly that the artistes had to wait in the artistes' room. Said Bjorn: 'There did not seem much point in arguing with him. We could not bear to watch the screen, but we had to go back into that boilerhouse of a room.'

Country after country cast its votes, with Katie Boyle overseeing the proceedings in Brighton, amazing the television audiences by flitting from language to language like a nonchalant butterfly. 'Waterloo' finally scored twenty-four points, six clear of the Italian entry 'Si', with the Dutch entry 'I See A Star' limping in third.

'We had won, and I couldn't believe it!' said Benny. 'We jumped around and hugged each other in our excitement. Anni-Frid looked as if she was going to faint. Bjorn started frantically searching for his guitar, the one that looked like a five pointed star, because we had to go back onstage for the traditional repeat of the winning song. He couldn't find it. Panic! Then it turned up, hidden behind a chair.'

Said Anni-Frid: 'The television cameras were on us all the time in that room, so a large part of Europe saw exactly how it was for us and how we felt. I would hate to have to go through those minutes again. I was so strained, I thought I must pass out. When we heard the announcer say we had won, we could hardly believe our ears. I just went numb, and I have only a haze-like, dreamy recollection of what happened next. My thoughts were completely scrambled, and in the middle of it all I felt ecstatic about the win. But I can't tell you if I was laughing or crying. It's a blur.'

The airtight security net tripped up the next stage of the contest. A guard by the stage knew that Stikkan Andersson was the author of 'Waterloo'. What he did not know was that his co-authors were Benny and Bjorn. And when they tried to follow Stikkan on to the stage to collect their trophy with him, the guard barred their way. Bjorn tried to explain, but the guard kept telling him that only the songwriter, and not the artistes, could go onstage during this presentation. 'In the end, I gave up, and figured that I could pick up the trophy later,' recalls Bjorn. 'I was a bit upset that we could not go on with Stikkan, but when I thought about it later, it struck me as rather funny. I don't blame the security guard. They had a difficult job on their hands in that auditorium, with people going all over the place. It must have been a nightmare trying to keep tabs on everybody.'

Benny managed to get past the guard and bounded on to join Stikkan. He said: 'I looked round for Bjorn, and saw him waving his arms at me as the guard barred his way. He looked a bit frantic at first, but then I saw him grinning and shrugging his shoulders. I know he felt a little bit cheated, but

I don't think he let it worry him. Me, I felt so happy I couldn't believe it, but before I knew what was happening, I was called to join the others and we were back onstage to do "Waterloo" again. We really gave it all we got, and I felt we were putting it over even better than we had for the contest performance.'

As the television pictures faded out from The Dome, a horde of press photographers invaded the stage to line Abba up for the photographs which were to go round the world. Then the group were hustled into an interview room to face a barrage of questions. What do you think about winning? What will you do now? Are you the first of a new wave of Swedish groups? The staccato questions were fired as fast as they could answer them.

Anni-Frid said: 'I've never seen so many reporters and photographers gathered together. They were quite a formidable sight. Questions came from every angle, and on just about every subject, I think. I really only have vague memories of the questions, and I've got no idea what answers we gave. It was all going to quickly, and my mind was struggling to catch up with what had happened.'

Said Benny: 'I think there were about 150 journalists and photographers for us to face. We had no idea who was asking what question; I remember there was a lot of laughter, and we were over the moon with happiness. I suppose this was the start of our victory celebration. When I read what we had said in answer to the questions, I put it down to the fact that the fast-moving confusion of the win had overtaken us.'

It was midnight before they could get away from the persistent questions and requests of the photographers. They went back to their hotel to shower and change their clothes before they headed back to The Dome. There, the mayor of the town came on to the stage and offered the four a free week in Brighton. 'We must take him up on that some day,' said Benny. 'Just as soon as we have the time.'

The non-stop whirl of the evening continued. The company which markets the Abba records in Germany threw a party for them, which they went along to. 'We drank a lot of champagne,' said Benny. 'It was fantastic. And we were to drink a lot more champagne in the next few days. I didn't mind at all.'

At four a.m. the two couples managed to break away and get back to their hotel. Said Bjorn: 'This was the calm after the storm. We could hear the silence after the pandemonium of the evening. We were so excited, but it's strange that at a time like that, you have nothing to say. How can you express your happiness?'

Benny and Anni-Frid, just along the corridor, felt exactly the same. 'Suddenly the crowd was gone, and we were on our own. I stretched out on the bed to relax, but it was very difficult to do so. I could feel the tingling excitement still flowing through me. Yes, it was a very strange feeling. And another strange thing was the name of our suite. The Napoleon Suite. Yes, that's true. What an incredible coincidence.'

The next day started with the ritual reading of the newspapers, to see what the critics had to say about the win. Some were chastening. Others were more warming. One unenlightened writer, mentioning that the Scandinavian and Dutch competitors sang in English, said: 'Surely it would have been more respectful to have them sing in their own languages.' If he thought the contest was an exercise in international friendship, he was very confused about idealism, which he obviously wanted to inject into it. He had been unable to assay the rich commercial vein running through the competitors' motivation. Richard Last of the *Daily Telegraph*, noting that they were the first *group* to win the contest, said: 'The Andersson formula proved a winner. It was certainly helped by the highly professional performance of the Abba group and the presence as lead singer of one of those archetypal Swedish blondes, seemingly all legs and hair. It used to be said that you could concoct a successful Eurovision song by correctly programming a computer. The programme will have to be changed, however, for the contest has taken a lurch, if not forward, at least sideways. This year, for the first time, there were four genuine pop groups in the ring, complete with drum kits and backing tracks, and the international jury, rejecting such conventional ballad banalities as Britain's "Long Live Love", awarded them two of the top three places. Even more encouragingly, they gave second place to a haunting Italian entry of above average musical interest which I had written off as "too good to win".'

The cynic who had wanted them to sing in Swedish, conceded: 'It was obvious that certain inroads had been made into Eurovision this year by groups, as opposed to solo artists, and, although the contest seemed even more synthetic than usual, their songs had the highest musical sensibility. As nation after nation coughed up its doubtful talents for an audience enveloped in a temporary cocoon of unreality, one pondered the grey conservatism that could produce such huge acceptance, far greater than any other music programme; one also pondered on the record companies in twenty countries who were lending their ears; on the original 7,000 songs from which the final entries were chosen – what on earth were THEY like?'

Incredibly, the newspaper really caught unawares by the Abba win was *Expressen* of Stockholm. The largest evening paper in Sweden made no preparations to cover a win by Abba. They were really caught with their pants down. After all, they seemed to reason, Swedish groups don't win competitions of this kind, do they? They did have the head of the paper's entertainment department over for the final, but, as far as they were concerned, he was only there to report the event, and presumably Abba losing graciously. Stikkan Andersson had told them repeatedly that he thought his group were going to win, but they had reached the stage where they took his 'We are the greatest' speeches with a very large pinch of salt. When Abba won, the *Expressen* office got into a bit of a panic; they did not know what to do. Their man in Brighton did not know enough about the Abba background to write the story for them, and they had no-one in the office who could handle it. They had not envisaged this problem arising because they, in common with most people in Sweden, could see no possibility of them winning. They just took a shrugging-the-shoulder attitude to the contest and figured that as long as they had someone in Brighton, that man would be able to write about what happened.

Peter Himmelstrand, co-author of this book, had been their music columnist until eighteen months previously. They called his home to ask him to write the major story they wanted to carry on Abba. His first reply was: 'No, I'm not specially interested in doing it, because I left that field when we decided I'd spent enough of my life writing about music.'

They appealed: 'We don't have anybody to write about them. The people working in your old field just don't know enough about Abba.' They were calling on him because he was the only member of their staff who had known and watched the members of Abba from their early days.

'I agreed, and had to stop a party I was giving at home in mid-flight, send my guests home, and go down to the newspaper office to write the stories about the members of the group.'

The *Expressen* coverage spread over three whole pages of the paper. It amounted to a revelation to the staff of the newspaper as well as to the readers. Both had no idea that the Abba win was even remotely on the cards. This was strange, because Sweden had been in the contest for a number of years. Or perhaps that was the reason no-one there gave them much of a chance. Perhaps they thought if they had not had a sniff of a win in all that time, they were never going to win. Perhaps it is a matter of a prophet not being recognised in his own country. Though, in fact, those in the music business knew they had a good chance of winning, and that they had it in them to make an international group. But those who felt that were a very tiny and select minority indeed.

The *Expressen* report was a jingoistic attempt to whip up Swedish fervour. It claimed: 'All Sweden cheered tonight for Abba.' But most Swedish people still considered that it was a big yawn. They thought it must be some fluke happening. They still had this feeling that anything Swedish can't really be of world shattering importance.

CHAPTER TWELVE

# A TRAIL OF CHAMPAGNE

Abba shrugged off the barbed carping of the critics and hit the champagne trail to celebrate their win. It started the day after the contest with a champagne breakfast, thrown for them by their British record company, CBS.

'I've never seen so much champagne as I did in those few days after the final,' says Anni-Frid. 'It was incredible. But I didn't complain at all. The bubbles in the glasses seemed to be shouting greetings to success and happiness, and we were experiencing both.'

The press corps was with them all the way for the first couple of days, and the group did hundreds of interviews and posed for an endless stream of photographs. Said Benny: 'The photography was starting to get to us. Stand this way. Stand that way. Look over here. Smile. It was a bit tiring, and at one time my face was fixed in a permanent smile which I thought I would never be able to get rid of. But we knew it was all part of the job, and tried not to be tiresome ourselves. Anyway, it was easy for us to look happy for the photographers, because we felt so much on top of the world that I'm sure the happiness radiated from us, and was there for everyone to see. We were bursting with it.'

Bjorn confessed. 'If I am to be absolutely honest, I must admit that we never thought we were going to win when it came to the actual contest. We talked about our rivals, and we felt sure the juries around Europe would go for the Dutch couple, Mouth and McNeil, with their lovely song "I See A Star". Of all the others in the final, we liked them the best ourselves, and to us it seemed inevitable that they would be collecting the trophy. So, when we won, it was a really splendid and warming moment for us to have Mouth and McNeil the first people to come up and congratulate us. They said they thought the best song and the best group had won, which I thought was very gracious and generous of them. Especially when you remember that they must have been feeling really disappointed themselves. For they had started out that day as second favourites to walk out winners. In fact, our reactions ranged from disbelief to exhaustion. Agnetha said she felt she had lost all contact with reality, and was floating in a dream somewhere. Anni-Frid was so knocked out she couldn't think at all. Benny and I refused to believe it was true. We were waiting for someone to come round and say: "Sorry, but we counted wrong. You haven't won after all." Of course, the count was not wrong, and we turned to face the stunning truth that we had won. Then came the really hard part, to go back onstage and sing again. We had been standing there entranced while the votes came in; we wanted to run away, but we couldn't. In a strange way, it was horrible. I could feel the tension crawling under my skin, and tingling in my stomach. And our mouths were so dry you wouldn't believe it. And immediately after that, we had to sing again. But I think we rose to it, and people who saw that part of the show congratulated us on coming back so well. It was just will driving us on. We were so exhausted, it was all we had left. Then I had something very important to attend to. For some reason which I cannot now imagine, my trousers had been made up wrong; they were so tight that I could not sit down in them, and for six hours, part of the time with my legs feeling as if they were going to give way under me, I could not sit down. So as soon as I got back to the hotel, they came off. The relief was incredible.'

When the press corps left town, Bjorn, Benny, Agnetha, and Anni-Frid were able to relax and get some peace and quiet. They settled down to read the three hundred congratulatory telegrams. Said Benny: 'After the electric tension of the past couple of days, we were able to breathe easily and start coming down to earth. We conquered the Napoleon

Suite with champagne and started to laugh the tension away. It was so odd. Everything seemed funny, and raised chuckles from us. I think it was just relief that it was all over. Nobody in the gang said one serious word during the whole day. I could not understand why none of us felt tired. After all that, surely we should have been exhausted? But we were not. I managed to get to sleep for a couple of hours in the afternoon, then in the evening the four of us went out for a meal. And what a meal! Grilled lobster and champagne. It's not everybody who has a dinner like that. This was the life.

'The telegram reading had produced some great moments. At that time Anni-Frid and I were living in an area near Stockholm known as Vallentuna, and the local kommun – the Swedish equivalent to a local council – had sent their greetings. And so, amazingly, had the Swedish Royal Navy. That's a telegram we have really treasured.'

On the Monday, Benny took a stroll from his hotel to mark another victory. Over the local bookmaker. He recalls: 'He was a great guy. He seemed so happy for me, and he congratulated me, too. What a way to pay out your winners!'

Later, the group were driven up to London in a limousine, and on the way were delighted to hear 'Waterloo' playing on the car radio. 'It was so strange, it seemed as if we were listening to someone else playing,' said Bjorn. 'We all agreed that we were delighted the contest had been held in England, where everything was so well organised, where everyone was interested in what was happening, and where they were so courteous to us.'

At their London hotel they found more champagne waiting for them, two bottles in each room. Stikkan came in to say that they were wanted to appear on BBC Television's Top of the Pops programme that week. 'We'll do this one,' said Stikkan. 'But from here on in we'll be looking very carefully at the offers coming our way, and deciding for ourselves precisely which ones we are going to accept and which we are going to refuse. We're top of the pile at the moment, and they are going to be courting us.' He was immediately tested by two telephone offers: one from a promoter in New York, the other from the Swedish owner of a tiny travelling Tivoli fairground. Both got the same reply from Stikkan: 'Thank you for thinking of us, but, at the moment, no thank you.' There were many other offers to look at, and Stikkan was already planning their year ahead from those, plus a few ideas of his own.

Benny retired to his room, where he passed the evening watching an old horror movie on television. 'A strange old-fashioned film it was, but isn't it amazing how, at times of tension, they are so relaxing,' says Benny. 'I was totally enthralled.'

A small gloom cloud appeared, in the form of Agnetha, who complained of a pain in her throat. She said: 'I have been plagued with tonsilitis since I was a kid, and I knew this was the same old problem on its way again. I could feel the giddiness and the yuckiness coming over me. But in the midst of all that, I said a little prayer of thanks that it had not come a couple of days before. Imagine getting a throat infection on the day of the contest! I shudder when I think that could have happened – and ruined our chances.'

The group had before them a few days to sample the delights of London, a city which still retains the swinging image of the 1960s for Europeans. Benny and Anni-Frid went out shopping and made the obligatory journey down to the King's Road, legendary centre of London of the Swinging Sixties. Anni-Frid bought a dress there. 'It's a continuing source of amazement to me that styles there always seem so far ahead of everywhere else,' she said. But she was in for a surprise when she and Benny stopped at a pub for a beer. She said: 'The pub was jammed to the doors, so Benny suggested we stand on the pavement to have our drink. I said, "You can't do that." For that sort of thing is unimaginable in Sweden, where drinking is not the same sort of social event that it is in England. But when I saw some other people edge out of the pub to drink on the pavement, too, I realised this was a familiar tradition here. So we had our drinks out there, too, just like the others. We really felt part of the scene, and, do you know, it was fun. Standing there, with our beers in our hands, watching the world go by. Now I understand why so many people do it. It's very relaxing.'

Bjorn was a little shocked by the drinking habits of the English. 'I find myself spending half the time refusing yet another beer. It's incredible. I don't know how they do it. In Sweden, it's usual to have a drink on a Friday or Saturday night, but here they drink all the time. It's something I had to see to believe.'

Benny found himself a snakeskin jacket then the couple returned to team up with Agnetha and Bjorn for another encounter with the press, who took them to Hyde Park for a photography session. The Swedish ambassador in London, Ole Jodahl, and eight proud members of his staff turned up to add their congratulations. He said: 'This is my proudest day in England. I think your group has done a fine job in spreading goodwill. You are fine ambassadors yourselves.'

The busy whirl of London continued with an interview by disc jockey David Hamilton at the BBC. It did not help Agnetha, who felt worse than ever.

Benny recalls: 'For some reason I cannot explain, none of us could manage to sleep well in London. I spent hours walking round the room and looking out of the window on to Hyde Park. Perhaps it was nerves keeping us all awake. I suppose once you reach the pitch that we did during the contest in Brighton, it takes a while to come down. It was happening painfully slowly for us.

'Agnetha developed a fever, but she's a great girl and she would not let it stand in the way of her joining Bjorn and the rest of us for another BBC interview. We told her that if she felt so rotten, she should stay in bed, but she insisted that she was going to pitch in and do her bit.

'She kept with us all the way, and this was a very busy few days. The London *Daily Express* came along to take us to Waterloo Station for some photographs. They wanted us dressed as flamboyantly as possible, so I selected a sequined white silk jacket. Then we were whisked off to the BBC Television Centre in Shepherds Bush to record our spot on Top of the Pops. What a great programme that is! We don't have anything like it in Sweden. The only night of the year in Sweden that the kids can listen to a lot of pop music is when the Eurovision Song Contest is shown which means, of course, only one night a year. How marvellous it would be if we could have a programme like Top of the Pops.

'I wasn't surprised that with all the dashing around, Agnetha felt worse than ever. But she still would not give up. We think she was feeling really yucky because of all that penicillin and anti-biotics which had been pumped into her. Despite that, the recording went very well and she didn't show a glimmer of how she must have felt inside. I really felt for her, and I was also very grateful to her for putting up with all the agony for us.

'After the recording at the BBC, I remember someone asking me if I didn't get fed up with singing "Waterloo" all the time. I told them that, on the contrary, I enjoyed it more every time. That's curious, isn't it? But that's how it is.'

The cream of Europe's pop journalists were impressed at the way Bjorn took command in the mass interviews and controlled the situation. But, at one of the receptions in their Park Lane Hotel, Benny took centre stage to say: 'It has been champagne all the way since Brighton, including champagne with our cornflakes. Sunday was out of this world as no one said a serious word.

'It's been just fantastic. I mean, the fact that we are sitting here talking to all you people shows what the contest has done for us. It's obviously a very big thing for us. Back home the reaction to our success has been tremendous.

'We thought we had a good song, though we also thought maybe it was a little out of style for the Eurovision Song Contest. But it turned out everything went fine. Olivia Newton-John's song was too similar to your previous entries, and that was the problem with a lot of the other entries. Our style is what was needed.

'It's a strange fact of life that in Sweden, people have not looked on us as a group in the way they look on Mud or The Sweet. That's because people have known us before and followed our earlier careers. Perhaps now they will think of us as a group.'

There was another English ritual for Bjorn and Agnetha to face before they left London. A meeting with a calligrapher, who was to try to test their character from their handwriting. Bjorn, he assessed, was extravagant and shy, and gentle. Agnetha, on the other hand, liked meeting people and was more practical, he said. Bjorn's reaction to this was: 'The fellow must have got our handwriting samples mixed up, because his assessment of Agnetha matched me and his weighing up of me matched Agnetha.'

Bjorn was more pleased by the questions the journalists were asking them. He said: 'In Sweden, we are always being asked about politics. Now, what on earth do I know about politics? It's a mystery world to me. I'm just a guy who writes happy songs. What has that got to do with politics? That fact does not deter the questionners in Sweden. They want to know if we're Socialists, if we believe in democracy, and so on. I tell them that I don't know what they mean by those terms. We have a democracy at work in the group, and we always talk about our plans before any decision is made. And that means all the decisions. Like what clothes we'll wear. And, particularly, about my long hair. There's no messing about with this. I am tired of having it long and I would like to get it cut. But we have had long discussions about this between all of us, and we decided that I look better onstage with long hair. So, okay, I agreed to keep it. That's democracy.'

Which reminds Agnetha about a hairy problem she had to face up to at this time. 'I also wanted to have my hair clipped short,' she said. 'This is because my hair needs frequent washing, takes ages to dry, and comb, and keeps getting in my way. That is if it's long. And just before the Eurovision Song Contest final I made up my mind absolutely and irrevocably that I would have it cut very short. Then our photographs started going all over the world – featuring me with my hair long. That hair had become part of our image, and, whether I liked it or not, it was going to have to stay.

'I would like to say that I'm delighted I did keep it long. The effect of long, dark hair, especially when we are performing, say, in Italy or Spain is sensational. Blondes with waist-length hair are obviously a rarity in those countries, and if I even walk along the street, you should see the commotion it creates. So it must stay as it is – except I shall probably start plaiting it when I'm not in the public eye. The care I have to take over it still drives me wild.'

As for Bjorn, he is delighted about her hair. He said: 'I know how she feels, but I'm glad she is keeping her hair long. I think it looks beautiful.'

The critics who liked Abba felt they were going to make a monumental impact on pop music. The well known lyric-writer Harold Spiro said: 'Abba is blowing a wind of change through the pop world. I think that because of their win in Brighton, almost every country will enter a group for the contest next year.' And in London a few days after the win, Stikkan Andersson announced: 'We can't grow much more in Sweden, and now we must look to the international market. But we are also going to handle that very carefully. We have had an enormous number of offers, including a number for work in the United States. We are going to consolidate ourselves first in Europe and Australia, who are taking to us now. We will only go to the United States for a concert tour when we think the time is good and ready, and not a minute before.' Stikkan also had a few words to say about the selection system in Sweden which had kept Abba out of the final the year before. He said: 'When the archaic system was swept away, it opened up the door to what people wanted. This year it was the ordinary people of Sweden and Europe who decided the winner, and that's why we won. "Waterloo" is a song for the people.'

Pop writer Rosemary Horide could also see a transformation of the Eurovision contest. She wrote in *Disc* magazine: 'The Eurovision Song Contest is dead. Long live the new Eurovision Song Contest. The aforementioned sad event occurred on Saturday, 6 April, 1974, in sun city, Brighton, Sussex. Seventeen songs were competing and sixteen were within the general Boom Bang A Puppet In A Box formula. Each may have had certain individual merits, but they were recognisable as that peculiar entity – A Eurovision Song. Then something went wrong. The one different song won. It was performed by four young people dressed *á la* Glitter – an unusual contrast to the evening dress of most of the other competitors. The group were a Swedish band called Abba. They'd obviously taken the dressing-up seriously – even their conductor was wearing a Napoleonic costume, complete with hat. The song was called "Waterloo" and owned one of the most peculiar sets of lyrics it's ever been my pleasure to encounter. You may not have been able to decipher them, so here's a sample: "My, my at Waterloo Napoleon did surrender, Oh Yeah, and I have met my destiny, In quite a similar way." The formidable combination of that song and the costumes won the hearts of the international panel of judges, who voted it into the winning position. And that was the end of the Eurovision Song Contest as we know it. Why? Well, the whole concept of Sweden's entry was so different from the Eurovision norm. As it won, it seems inevitable that we've said goodbye to the old-style winning songs, and the contest has been dragged, protesting, into the '70s. From now on, hopefully, the songs chosen will bear some relation to the rest of contemporary popular music. And that could also change the various countries' choice of artists, which would mean a facelift, if not a complete re-incarnation for Eurovision.'

A sour note was sounded, however, by rivals who were angry because Abba had used backing tracks on their Brighton presentation, and had been pretending to play their instruments. They were by no means unique in this, for all the other groups performing had pre-recorded their music for the contest. But a number of soloists protested, and the Portuguese singer Paulo de Carvalho said: 'I think everything should be "live" for everyone – it would be fairer. It's not right that groups do not come on stage and perform their music with their singing in this contest. This is not artistry. I have to sing with an orchestra that is playing at that very moment, and anything could go wrong.'

But a BBC production chief explained: 'It's in the rules of the contest that backing tracks may be used as long as they are instrumental only and all the people who played on the backing track appear on stage. Technically, it would make the show more difficult if we had to wait for groups to set up and balance their equipment.'

Another sour note came from Britain's entrant, Olivia Newton-John, who said of her song, 'Long Live Love': 'It's not the sort of song I'd choose personally if I was looking for a new single, but it's a good Eurovision song.' Of the bumpetty-bump toe-tapper, with lyrics about the Salvation Army, she said: 'I knew all along it was unsuitable. It was very frustrating having to go through those rehearsals when the song wasn't right. I wouldn't have chosen it. I'd have preferred a ballad.'

Music critics felt the British selection panel had made a mistake. One said: 'By choosing a bomp-a-bomp formula song with the usual waltzlike feel they failed to match the products of the more enlightened Europeans like Holland, Israel, Yugoslavia, and Sweden, whose victory was a victory for ingenuity.' However, Miss Newton-John was compensated, despite finishing only in fourth place, with a three-year world-wide recording deal.

Stikkan Andersson was not overpleased, either, with a 3 a.m. call from a Swedish television reporter who telephoned him to ask for an interview, then launched it with the question: 'Are you aware of the fact that forty thousand people died during the battle of Waterloo?'

Said an exasperated Stikkan: 'I thought I was going to faint. Don't these people know anything? Don't they know that Waterloo is a symbol, another word for defeat? That you can use it instead of the word defeat?'

Then came the time to bid a fond farewell to England. They had enjoyed their visit, and were grateful for the gigantic boost to their career. But Agnetha, for one was glad to be heading home. She said: 'The hardest part of the travelling is leaving my daughter, Linda, behind. I always miss her on these trips, and, much as I may be enjoying myself, there's always that background nagging thought that I want to get back to her. Fortunately, we have a wonderful nanny to look after her when we're away. But I'm always glad to get back.'

They were all ready to go home. But first they had another date to keep, for a television show in Hamburg, Germany. The sang 'Waterloo' – again, and in a studio which was crammed with goats, chickens, and rabbits, brought in for an Easter show. Almost without breaking stride, they headed back to Hamburg Airport to catch an ongoing plane to Stockholm. Benny and Anni-Frid passed the flight with a game of chess – and Anni-Frid won, for the first time since they had started playing together a few months before. At Arlanda Airport, twenty miles outside Stockholm, there was no-one to meet their plane when it touched down a few minutes before midnight. 'That was fine by us,' says Benny. 'In fact, it was a bit of a relief. After all the hustle and bustle of the last few days, it was nice to have a quiet, ordinary arrival. No-one had turned up because we were not expected back in Sweden until Friday, the next day. But it was not a matter of us trying to slip back into town and avoiding everybody. It was sheer chance, even if it was a very welcome one for us. Anni-Frid and I drove home to our place just a short way from Bjorn and Agnetha's house in Vallentuna, and I can tell you it was a great pleasure to be able to relax and be entirely ourselves, and to be alone, really alone, for the first time for a couple of weeks. We shared another bottle of champagne and sat and talked about what had happened in Brighton, about what we thought of London, about what it was like to be back. We talked on and on and on for hours. It's amazing we had so much to talk about, because we had, after all, been together all the time. But that's the way Anni-Frid and I are. We always seem to be able to find something to talk about, and usually quite a lot.'

Agnetha had the pleasure of gazing at baby Linda in bed. 'I wanted to pick her up and hug her, but I thought she would prefer it if I left that till the morning,' said Agnetha.

The next day, the Abba team – Bjorn and Agnetha with Linda, Benny and Anni-Frid, and Stikkan with his wife and three children – headed for the place they had been dreaming of all the time they were in Brighton: the island out in the archipelago outside Stockholm which they shared with about twenty other families. 'For me, it felt that I was free at last,' said Benny. 'This island was where we did all our best work, composing and writing. It's amazing what a bit of time hidden from the crowd can do for your creative urge. We can all relax there. We go for walks in the forest, work in the garden, go fishing. We don't catch any fish, of course, but that isn't the object of fishing, is it? That's how we spent Easter, just relaxing and not being forced to do anything. We all had a fantastic time.'

CHAPTER THIRTEEN

# AT HOME

Abba came back home bubbling with happiness. But, with every victory there have to be casualties. Their win in Brighton was to spell defeat for thousands of Swedes who had hoped to see their conquering heroes in a scheduled tour of the *folkparks* in that summer of 74. For, with offers flooding in from all over the world in the wake of their Eurovision triumph, they decided to cancel the tour.

Stikkan Andersson wrote a letter of apology to the managers of the thirty *folkparks* they had planned to appear in, explaining that their new commitments made it impossible for them to spend July on the tour. Plans were so far advanced that Abba had even given their detailed instructions about stage design; they were able to drop out because no-one in the Abba organisation had actually signed the necessary contract. Stikkan told the managers: 'They are very tired, and Benny and Bjorn have important work to do as producers for the other artistes in the Polar Company. They also have an LP of songs to write, and this task alone is going to take them six months. July is their only chance to get some rest in a long time.'

A howl of protest from all sides met his decision. The *folkparks* managers considered taking Abba to court, and newspapers all over the country urged that they should go ahead with the tour. The *folkparks* management said: 'Their decision is immoral. They have deserted us and the audiences.'

A reporter asked if it was not foolish to cancel the tour, and if they were not worried about angering the audiences. Stikkan's answer was: 'What do you want us to do? We have a chance to launch an international career in the wake of "Waterloo". Would you have us pass that up to sing in the parks? When London calls us and says: "Fly over here to appear on television", do you really expect us to say: "Sorry, we can't, because we have to appear in some tiny town in Sweden"?' Stikkan was to add, while in Paris for a television show. 'It is important for Abba's future that we do a concert tour of Europe rather than a tour of the Swedish *folkparks*. It disappointed us to miss the tour, but to work for small fees in the *folkparks* when Europe is waiting to be conquered would not make sense.'

Bjorn said: 'We have all discussed this carefully with Stikkan, and the decision has been the decision of us all. A month on tour in the parks would mean a month out of rehearsal time, and we can't spare it. We must think of the other artistes in the organisation, who we have to do work for. We also have to think of our own health, and make sure we don't overdo it. No-one will lose any money because of our decision. The musicians who would have played with us will get other jobs. What is upsetting us is that we have to let down our Swedish audiences. But we are sure they will forgive us, and we are hoping to do a show in Sweden later this autumn.'

So, instead of going round the *folkparks*, Abba spent part of the summer in Europe, on a back-breaking itinerary, which took them in triumph through radio and television programmes in Britain, France, Holland, Germany, and Belgium. Their fans in Sweden had to wait till the next year before they were treated to shows by their group. Abba did a one-hour show in the giant Stockholm Tivoli, and followed this up with a July tour of the *folkparks*, a tour which took them to fourteen venues in three weeks. This, they said, was to make up for the previous year. But even this tour did not go according to plan, and was nearly lost at the last moment. On the day they were to set out, Agnetha had another attack of her throat trouble, developed a fever, and the tour had to be postponed for a week. They completed the tour, to tumultuous receptions from their fans, but not without another dose of criticism. Stikkan Andersson had asked for, and got, a percentage of the 'take' at each *folkpark*. He countered with the argument: 'Abba aren't ordinary Swedish artistes. They are international artistes, and for that sort of talent, it is only fair that people should pay. If we can draw big crowds to the *folkparks*, why shouldn't we get our fair share of the receipts? And it is computed on a percentage basis, so we are taking as much risk as the *folkparks*.'

The Abba victory also presented someone else with an unexpected dilemma. Tradition in the Eurovision Song Contest holds that the winning country is accorded the honour of hosting the next year's competition. When executives of Swedish Television heard about 'their' group winning, they threw their hands up in despair. 'We'll never be able to manage it,' they said. 'A small country like us is just not equipped for this sort of thing.' This protest didn't hold much water. After all, hadn't tiny Luxembourg managed to host the contest. If they could, anybody could. So, though Swedish Television tried to buck the tradition, they realised that, of course, they could hold the contest, and it was duly scheduled for Stockholm the next year.

Abba's feet did not touch the ground that summer. They had offers of work which would have kept them busy twenty-four hours a day. Most of it they had to turn down. Said Bjorn: 'Remember, we also have a lot of work to do in the studio for the other artistes Benny and I produce records for. There is no-one else who can get the effect they want on their records. We can't let them down. We are also concentrating on our own studio work. We are going to have to devote a lot of time on that, or there will not be any new Abba records for next year. We're not a group who can go into a studio and slam out a record. It takes us a considerable, in fact an enormous amount of preparation and hard work before we get the result that we are all happy about. We're really perfectionists in that way, and by the time we get a record out of the way, we are left pretty much drained of energy and we have to dash back to our island, not to work, but to get our feet up, breathe some fresh air, and rest. When we're in full flow of working, we're all very much on edge and it takes a lot out of us. All that energy has to be replaced, ready for the next bout with the creative urge.'

The problem of what to do with all the extra money they were going to make did not daunt them at all. Said Benny: 'We've already got some very nice houses and our places on the island. We keep very much to ourselves and we enjoy the simple things in life. You know, a can of beer and a soccer match on the television. That's fine for me. I don't think our lives will change very much at all. Not because of the money. There's not so much we want, you know.'

Bjorn agreed: 'Our lives are going to change because we will be working very much in the international circuit now. Brighton has done that for us, and we are very grateful for it. It's given us a big boost, a giant step forward, and it may open the door to the United States for us. But on a private level, we do pretty well the same things now that we have over the past few years. We've got nicer places to live, but we're not trying to, and we're not interested in, living like princes.'

Even the Swedish newspapers, whose praise of Abba had been more than reserved, had to admit they were on their way to conquering Europe. 'Waterloo' jumped fifteen places in a week to sit at number two on the English charts. A jubilant Stikkan Andersson said: 'It's fantastic news. We can hardly believe it. Just think of it – number two in the so-called home of pop music!' The record blasted its way into the charts in ten European countries and was finally to sell more than five million. Months after Brighton, it was still riding high in the charts, and was number one in four countries.

Stikkan Andersson showed his master's touch by ordering that 'Ring, Ring', the Abba success of the previous year, should be released in England. As a follow-up to 'Waterloo', it zoomed into the charts. 'I think it was every bit as good as

"Waterloo" and, anyway, I thought it should have won the Eurovision Song Contest the year before,' he said. 'I really believe it would have, if it were not for the jury of experts who put it out of business.'

The summer saw Abba returning to London to launch 'Ring, Ring' with one of their spectacular appearances on Top of the Pops, where they have always put on a performance of class and style which put the efforts of other groups in the shadows, demonstrating how it should really be done. Unfortunately, on this occasion, they were to find that, in true British style, an industrial dispute had pulled the plug on the show. They went on to make a series of radio broadcasts, and the television dispute did nothing to halt the rise of their new British release.

Said Stikkan Andersson: 'I was so pleased when "Ring, Ring" did so well in the wake of "Waterloo". I know that many, many people – critics and others in the music business – said after we won at Brighton: "Okay, they won, but this is just a flash in the pan, a one-shot. They were fine, but that's the last we'll hear of them. It is the major challenge that faces anybody who wins the Eurovision Song Contest. Think back over the years to the names of the people who won. What have you heard from them since? Or can you even remember their names?" This was not going to happen to Abba, I vowed. But we were aware of the problems. It's one thing to win a Eurovision Song Contest, but it's much, much tougher to come back with a follow-up. That is the hardest part. To come back with something better. Others before us had tried, but they had never come up with anything afterwards to match their victory. A major difference with us, I believe, is that even without the contest, we were going to become a big international name. I'm sure of that. I'm not saying that the boost of five hundred million people watching us win wasn't a big factor on our road to success, but I am convinced it was in no way essential for us. You must remember that most people in America, Japan, and Australia have never even heard of the Eurovision Song Contest. To get into those markets, you have to do a little bit more than win what to them is an obscure contest.'

It was Stikkan who had cried onstage at Brighton, in front of those five hundred million people. He was making his own mark in the international pop world, and *Expressen* carried an incisive look at 'Mr Biz'. It said: 'Not many people have seen the heart of this hardworking, arrogant, hit maker. He has finally achieved his ambition to make number one in the hit world championship. He has written more than three thousand lyrics. He has music companies. He has record companies. He is proud of his business achievements. He is outspoken. He does not shy at talking about his own abilities. He is not smitten with false modesty. He believes in his own opinions. He gets sour sometimes and says a few things in anger on television, and now he has cried with happiness on television. But Stikkan Andersson is a big man in the showbusiness carousel. He is a clever music man, who has battled his way to the top. He was a fresh wind when he first came into the music business fifteen years ago, with his intuitive nose for finding and recognising new talent, and he's still as fresh now as he was then.'

All the members of Abba were proud that they had put Sweden on the world pop scene. They also shook the Swedish record business by selling 200,000 singles of 'Waterloo', and even more of the album under the same name. But they were disappointed that Swedish Television, which, under the mantle of state control, was loth to help the commercial record companies, even if this meant depriving the youngsters in the country of their chance to hear pop music and see pop artistes. Benny said: 'As far as television in Sweden is concerned, pop fans – and there are plenty of them – get a raw deal. There is nothing like Top of the Pops. Magazine programmes are usually the only outlet for pop, and it is very rare to have a pop concert on television. So the Eurovision Song Contest final is the night of the year for Swedish people who like pop and light music. Swedish pop fans are pressing for the Eurovision contest to be held in Stockholm next year, and we are all hoping it will be.'

Abba were back on a Swedish stage in January 1975, for the first time in nearly two years. The venue was the Stockholm Concert Hall, and, after their long absence from Swedish audiences, the group were very, very nervous. The fans had no such doubts. The house was full to capacity. Benny recalls their nervousness: 'Swedish audiences are, I think, a bit different from audiences in other parts of the world. I'm not sure why that is, perhaps it is the Swedish character. It's like that feel of having a cold, critical eye examining you.'

The enthusiasm of the reception washed away their nervousness, and their return was a triumph. The atmosphere and feeling of that night were admirably captured in a report in *Aftonbladet*: 'Now it's over, the Swedish opening of the international group Abba. The last notes of "Waterloo" died out, the stage is empty, and the audience is heading towards the exit. One young teenage girl is struggling to contain her tears. She has finally seen her idols. You can see the rock-rhythms are still pulsating through her. This girl was one of nearly nineteen hundred in the audience which filled up the concert hall last night. She and all the others can vouch for the fact that Abba have created their triumph, even in Sweden. Those who possibly thought the enthusiasm for Abba had faded are seriously mistaken. The group is more popular than ever. And better. In Brighton, nearly a year ago, it was good. Now they are at least a few classes better. When the history of the pop of the seventies is written, Abba will figure at the top. The group's American manager, Sid Bernstein, was present at the opening last night. After the show he said: "They are among the best in showbusiness right now." Okay, it's his job to talk like that, but there is no way you can miss the feeling that he is very, very impressed by Abba. Their stage show is fast, talented, technical, brilliant, and generous. Generous, because there is no let up, even for a second, during the ninety-minute show. Everybody worked till their last breath. Singing, playing, dancing, giving all of themselves. And the result is good. Somewhere at the beginning, I noticed an underlying feeling of uncertainty, but it quickly disappeared. Towards the end, the heat and the sound level was so strong that it could have competed with the World War Two invasion of Normandy. Of course, the show is built on "sure numbers". Old successes like "Waterloo", "Ring, Ring", "Hasta Manana", "Honey, Honey", and "He Is Your Brother", are mixed fluently with their new melodies. There are some ballads, but most of it is in strong rhythm style. Anni-Frid worked hardest. She wasn't still for one moment. She even go-go danced on a podium. But add to this an exquisite effort in lighting, with different coloured spotlights and shimmering lights, soap bubbles all over the stage in the finale, and you may perhaps get the picture of Abba today. There is one more detail which is essential for their success. That is the group's clothes. They are perfect for a show like this. There is Agnetha in her tight, white overalls with a green cape and feathers. She's nice, but difficult in the mornings, says her husband Bjorn. But she has also been named as the owner of the sexiest bottom in Europe. And there is Anni-Frid in white miniskirt and white boots. Bjorn in glittering stage clothes and high heeled boots. Benny in leopard-patterned jacket and, later, in a white one and red pants. It all looks good, and, in fact, it's a feast on the eye.'

This was to be a rare critical reaction to Abba from the Swedish press. Most of the other critics were to prove rasping and in no way complimentary.

As the helter-skelter rush for Abba's signature on contracts developed, Anni-Frid stepped momentarily out of the group to make an LP called 'Frida' – the name her friends know her by. It was a big success, and sold over 100,000. But Stikkan Andersson vetoed an offer to her to appear as a soloist on a television programme, because he reasoned that if she were *seen* working alone, it would disturb the image of the group. Said Anni-Frid: 'I was disappointed at first, but when Stikkan explained his objection, I could only agree with him.' She was asked if the solo record meant she was thinking of quitting Abba. She replied: 'Of course not, but we do reserve the right to work separately, too, if we want to. Abba can't last for ever, and it makes a lot of sense to lay the foundations for a return to a solo career if and when that time should ever come around. I can't see it even in the distant future, but it may be there somewhere. You must be prepared.'

Agnetha finally decided that she could not put up with her tonsils problem any more, and had them taken out. She said: 'Something had to be done. We came so near to missing out in Brighton because of them, and there was no way of knowing when the infection would strike again. It could be at any crucial moment, and I decided that in the interests of both myself and the others, they had to go. After the operation, I must admit that I wished I had not had it done. But I think that is a feeling which hits everybody who has the operation after they have passed from teenage. The pain was excruciating. And the operation itself was horrible. I had just a local anaesthetic, and I was aware of the surgeon at work all the time. All the time, I kept telling myself that I was doing what had to be done, and that it was all worth it. They have given me trouble since I was a little girl, and I know I should have had them out before, but it was just one of those things that I never seemed to have time to get round to. The risk of upsetting our careers was too much, and that meant I had to find time. Of course, even when they were gone, I had another nagging worry to face. Would the operation affect my voice in any way? That's the biggest problem facing a singer over throat operations. You never can really tell how your voice is going to come through it. For a few weeks after the operation, I didn't even speak, because I was so scared that some change might have taken place. Very nervously, I got round to speaking. Then I had to face the next big test. Singing. I thought perhaps my voice would be higher, and that might change the whole flavour of our presentation. I could not describe to you how pent-up I felt as I stood at the microphone in the studio for the first time after the operation, preparing to do a recording. As it turned out, I had nothing to worry about. There was absolutely no change at all. None. What a relief. And all those problems my tonsils had given me in the past, were now very much in the past. And good riddance to them!'

CHAPTER FOURTEEN

# BONANZA

Gold and platinum discs have cascaded on to Abba like confetti. The world's reaction has stunned them. They have outsold everybody in sight to become the most successful vocal team since The Beatles. Every Abba record has become a number one hit and sold in the millions. The group, which was labelled a 'flash in the pan success' by some critics after Brighton, has produced a mind-boggling flow of hits which is reaching a flood tide. After 'Waterloo' they confirmed their staying power with 'Ring, Ring', 'I Do, I Do', 'Mamma Mia', 'Fernando', 'Dancing Queen', 'S.O.S.', 'Honey, Honey', and 'Money, Money, Money'. They have had four number one hits in England, another four in Germany, and three in France. Australia has caught Abba Fever which makes Beatlemania look like a Sunday school social. Everything the group puts on the market there goes to number one, and at one time there were five Abba singles in the top ten. And, in a population of thirteen and a half million, 860,000 copies of the 'Best of Abba' LP were sold. Even this is likely to be surpassed by their latest LP 'Arrival', which attracted orders totalling 700,000 in just ten days. 'Waterloo' went into the United States charts within a few days of its release there as a single, and reached the top five. A string of charts entries have followed, and their LP 'Greatest Hits' is on its way to a 'gold' rating. 'Waterloo' has topped a sale of five million worldwide as a single and three million as an album. 'Fernando' has sold six million as a single. The 'Greatest Hits' LP is past the five million mark and still rising. 'Dancing Queen' hit the number one spot in ten countries. To date, their worldwide sales have zoomed over the forty million mark; their records are breaking records everywhere.

'It has taken our breath away,' said Stikkan Andersson. 'Years ago, I promised Bjorn and Benny that, with my help, they would carve a place of honour for themselves in the world, but even I never expected anything like this. People have been trying to explain why it has happened. I don't know why, and I don't think anybody will be able to put their finger on it.

'We clicked in Australia shortly after we won in Brighton. Now we are the biggest thing that ever happened in showbusiness there. It's unbelievable. At first, I couldn't believe it, but I have to now. Let me explain it to you this way. In Australia, a sale of 25,000 LPs is enough to win you a golden record. Well, recently we shipped 700,000 copies of the new album "Arrival" to Australia in two days. Soon, every second household there will have at least one of our LPs. 700,000 is a vast sale in America. For Australia, it is unimaginable.

'It's the same story all over Europe. Take Holland, where we are bigger than The Beatles ever were. And even little Denmark, where we sold 200,000 copies of "Arrival" in three weeks. In the same time we sold 560,000 copies in Sweden, in a population of only seven million. If that sort of sale were repeated, pro-rata to the population, we would chalk up a sale of something like twelve millions. We have clicked in Canada, where "Fernando" is near the top of the singles charts and climbing. But we are still waiting for the break to come in America. From what I can see – because our popularity is gathering there all the time – it is only a matter of time before that comes.'

When 'Waterloo' reached number seven in the United States, Bjorn announced: 'We will go to the States. We've had offers, but at the moment we don't have the time to do it because of our commitments in Europe.' They found time after their single 'S.O.S.' went over the million sale mark there, and appeared on television shows in New York, Las Vegas, and Los Angeles. 'We found two weeks in the middle of a very tight schedule,' said Bjorn. 'And, let me tell you, we didn't go for the tiny fees we got from the television companies for appearing. We did it to show ourselves and make contact with the people who buy our records.'

Sid Bernstein, the superpromoter who took The Beatles to America, and who is their American manager, predicted: 'Abba will be superstars in the States.' Their television appearances were seen by over a hundred million people. But Bjorn said: 'We are not ready to do a concert tour of America yet. We want to wait till we've had one or two more hits, then the tour will be on our terms.'

They opened and closed the Merv Griffin Show from the stage at Caesar's Palace in Las Vegas, where they were introduced as 'an international supermusic group'. But their tour was so hectic, they didn't really have time to see Las Vegas. Bjorn went out to buy a guitar and Benny could not resist losing a bit of money at blackjack. Agnetha and Bjorn had a special problem, which kept them awake at night. Baby Linda, who could not get used to the time change. 'It was okay for her,' said Agnetha. 'She was awake all night and slept during the day. But we had a lot of work to do in the day.'

Centre of attraction for the photographers were the girls, but Bjorn and Benny did not mind. Benny said: 'It's much more important that the girls are in focus. They look so much better than us.'

On the Dinah Shore Show in Los Angeles, Miss Shore made an offer to Benny and Anni-Frid, which they felt able to refuse. She said: 'I understand you two have been too busy to wed. Well, if you would like to marry here and now, you can do it in front of the television cameras, and in front of millions of Americans.' Later, Benny said: 'Anni-Frid and I are, of course, still engaged. We will get married when we have the time, and in the place we want to. Both of us felt that place was not on television. Not for us, anyway.'

Abba records are heard at frighteningly regular intervals all over the world, and every play brings them more income. Stikkan Andersson, who has done a lot of round the world travelling for Abba in the past three years, still gets a big kick when he turns up in a strange country and hears their records on radio. 'It's a wonderful feeling,' he said. 'I may be thousands of miles from home and in a country I have never visited before. Hearing the music takes me right back to Stockholm, and gives me that comforting "at home" feeling. And it happens everywhere, but everywhere, that I find myself.'

The group have no reservations about their love affair with Australia, where the people have taken Abba to their hearts with an enthusiasm unheard-of even amongst that volatile nation. A Sydney newspaper put it this way: 'This is the biggest thing to hit Australia since Tornado Tracey.' When the group arrived at Melbourne Airport, police had to be called in to control the frantic crowds of fans. Then Bjorn, Benny, Agnetha, and Anni-Frid had to be sneaked out through a garage so they could get to a television studio, where they were to record a show. The location of that studio had to be a closely guarded secret. 'Otherwise we were afraid the fans would take the place to pieces trying to get in,' said a harassed police chief. The resulting forty-five-minute special was watched by 58 per cent of the viewership, better figures than the moon landing, and an Australian record that Abba now share with Frank Sinatra. The five concerts they gave in Australia in October, 1976, were sold out the day the tickets went on sale. Stikkan Andersson and the group came in for some unique criticism in Australia. He recalls: 'This was because we made a momentous decision for a concert we had scheduled for Sydney, at the gigantic Showground stadium, which can hold forty thousand people. The tickets were sold without difficulty, but I was concerned about what some parents were saying; they didn't dare send their kids to a stadium jam-packed with so many people. So I decided we would have to cut the ticket sales. By half. That meant more benches could be put in, and more people could be seated, rather than have them crammed in, standing. And so that none of the ticket holders would miss out, we arranged to do two concerts to twenty thousand people rather than one to forty thousand. We had to play two concerts for the price of one, but it was more important to me to avoid that sort of feeling among parents. As a parent myself, I would never have sent my children to that place with forty thousand people crammed in. I felt that as soon as I saw the place, and realised what it would be like. So there was only one honest and sensible decision to make. Cut the crowd by half and make sure they would all be safe. Forget about the money, the people are more important than the money. We could have sold 80,000 for the two shows, but we were happy to sell 40,000. Our main purpose in being in Australia at all was to show our appreciation for what has happened there. We didn't want to celebrate our success with a crowd accident. That is how our philosophy goes. We are more interested in the people than the money. A similar thing happened at Gothenberg when we did a show in an auditorium which could hold 12,000 people. I told them to keep the numbers down to 9,000, because then everybody there would be able to see the show in comfort and listen to it in comfort. That's a lot better than finishing the day with 3,000 upset customers, complaining that they can't see or can't hear. That's no way to go on, there's no future in that.'

So popular have Abba become in Australia, that they have been accorded the ultimate accolade – pirated records. Police have taken possession of hundreds of thousands of LPs, copied from the originals, and sold inside black-and-white-photograph-covered sleeves. Pirate editions of their records have also turned up in Singapore, Hong Kong, Taiwan, and Italy. 'Accolade it may be, yes,' said Stikkan. 'I had never really thought of it that way, and it's the sort of tribute we would rather that people didn't pay us. If anybody is going to make a living out of Abba records, we would very much like it to be us, please.'

The Australia tours have been a rare diversion for Abba. They pick their shots carefully, and they don't plan to spend their lives doing one-nighters around the world. But they have made something of an exception for Britain, which they do like to visit. They put on the style in London to launch their LP, 'Arrival'. From London Airport, they flew in Abba-labelled helicopters – to match the helicopters on the cover of the album – and came in to a press reception at the Thames-side heliport. They went on to a welcoming pop-scene party on board a pleasure boat. There, BBC disc jockey Simon Bates presented them with an astonishing collection of thirty-two gold, platinum, and silver discs to acknowledge their phenomenal record sales in Britain.

'It is a continuing source of pleasure to us when we get these awards in Britain,' said Bjorn. 'Everywhere in the world, Britain is looked on as the home of modern pop music, particularly in relation to groups. For were The Beatles not the first of the great world-ranging groups? In fact, it was The Beatles and the song-writing of Paul McCartney and John Lennon which encouraged Benny and I to start writing pop songs when we did. We thought: "If they can do it, then so can we." '

A disappointment they found in England was the regular orchestra of the BBC programme Top of the Pops. Said Bjorn: 'We were not very happy with the support the orchestra gave us. I don't know exactly what it was, I find it hard to put my finger on it, but something was missing, and it just did not match our sound. So we started bringing our own musicians over with us for the recordings, and I think our appearances on the programme have shown a distinct improvement with their presence.'

Abba were also very careful about the arrangements – in a quite different respect – for their tour of Britain in February 1977, a tour which was a sell-out three months before they arrived in the country. They wrote to concert promoter Danny Betesh, responsible for the show at Manchester's council-owned Free Trade Hall, and asked if the money could be paid in German marks or Swiss francs. So the city council arranged to pay in marks; Betesh said: 'Obviously they felt that in sterling their money might be worth less after the concert. They were doing what many foreign businessmen are doing in these precarious days.'

The tour was, in fact, their first of Britain, though there had been a clamour for one since their Brighton win. Till then, Britain had always got the same reply Abba gave to German President Walter Schiels when he was giving a private reception for Gerald Ford, the visiting U.S. President. Schiels, an Abba fan, asked if the group could come along to entertain, but they had to turn him down, because they could not fit the reception into their hectic whirl of engagements, concerts, recordings, and production work. Said Bjorn: 'Nothing would have pleased us more than to perform for the two presidents, but it just was not possible, I'm afraid.'

The clamorous demand for Abba had infected the whole of Europe. The British tour is part of a world tour, which includes a stop in Copenhagen, where five thousand tickets were sold out in six hours, and the concert hall's switchboard broke down under the onslaught of calls. So Abba changed their plans, and decided to hold two concerts in the Danish capital to meet the demand.

A Munich radio station was flooded with calls of a more sombre nature. Thousands of kids wanted to ask about a rumour going round Germany that Abba had been in a plane crash, that three of them had died, the only survivor being Anni-Frid, who would not be able to sing again. The rumour had spread through Munich in no time at all, but all the while, the group were at home in Sweden. Benny's reaction was: 'This sort of thing always seems to spring up around groups. I remember rumours that The Beatles had died going round in the same way. I don't know why it happens. But news of our deaths was greatly exaggerated.'

Abba have taken Eastern Europe by storm in a way that no other group has. Their army of fans built up in Poland through kids there hearing Abba records on the Swedish and German radio broadcasts as well as their own radio programme. Then, when the Polish Prime Minister visited Sweden, a Polish newspaper published the address of the

Abba fan club in Stockholm. During the course of one week, this produced a flood of ten thousand letters from Polish Abba fans. And this was at a time when Poles could not even buy Abba records. Even the Polish government could not resist this sort of demand, and Abba were invited over for a twenty-four-hour visit to Warsaw in October 1976. The government laid on a Russian Illuysian jet aircraft, decorated with the Abba insignia, for their journey. To mark the first visit of a western pop group to an eastern European country, the authorities allowed fifty journalists and photographers to travel with them. A hundred Polish kids turned up at Warsaw Airport to greet Abba, who were driven into town in triumph to record a 'special' for Poland's state-run television network. The visit, organised by the Minister of Tourism, was a big success. So was their LP, 'Abba', which was released in Poland. It sold over 200,000 copies. Said Stikkan Andersson: 'We were there for a day and a night, and it was an incredible success. We are the biggest thing that has ever happened in Poland, Hungary, East Germany, and Czechoslovakia. At a press reception after the TV show, there were hundreds of journalists from Eastern Europe, and even from Tass, the Russian news agency. And the sale of 200,000 LPs was a fleabite compared to the number that could have been sold. Poland, like the other Eastern countries, has a currency exchange problem, and this was strictly a limited-issue record. I think we could have sold a million. I'm sure of that because our records there became like gold dust and were being sold on the black market for far more than the retail price. Normally, there is also a problem for Western artistes when it comes to bringing their earnings out of Communist countries, but these countries do have a certain quota of funds which can be spent on foreign musicians that the government there approves of. Obviously, they approved of us, and in a big way because they allocated all the next year's funds to us. It's an incredible situation, and we regard it as a great compliment.'

The East European journalists caught a few glimpses of the characters of the members of the group during the press conferences and photo sessions. Benny was asked if he knew any Polish musicians, and he replied. 'Yes, I dig this Chopin group.' And when the group were made to march up and down the aircraft steps, like the Duke of York's men, for repeated photographs, an irritated Anni-Frid snapped: 'Up or down? Make up your mind!'

Said Stikkan: 'The Polish television viewers, like so many others around Europe, would have seen us first on the Eurovision Song Contest. They also have their own voting programmes, where they play records and vote for them. And there has been an intriguing development since Poland. The Russian youngsters have started knocking at the Abba door. Russian listeners have heard us on Polish radio, and they want us there, too. So we have started negotiations with the Russians with a view to going there. Our "Abba" LP has been released there – 25,000 copies were sent from our West German record company, Polydor. It is unheard of for pop groups to have records released in Soviet Russia, because the Russian authorities usually frown on pop music. How the market will develop there I can't say, but I do know that the allocation for our next record release in Poland stands on the 800,000 mark.'

Abba are very much their own masters. They are never told what to do by anyone. They work when and where they choose and they record the material *they* want. And nobody can drag them out of Sweden for more than a few weeks at a time. They don't aim to get caught in the touring trap. Said Benny: 'We are headed for Britain in February, and following up with an Australian tour in March, but these are exceptions. Normally, we only do television promotion, though we do occasional concerts, and enjoy doing them. The trouble is, it's very expensive for us to do concerts, because there are eighteen of us on stage – four or five keyboard players, two guitarists beside Bjorn, two boys and two girls in the choir, bass, drums, and a percussionist. A pretty expensive entourage.' With or without tours, Abba are on a worldwide hit-trail, but Benny admits to a nagging problem: 'At the moment I feel we need more up-tempo numbers to balance out what we do onstage. It's difficult for us to write up-tempo numbers because there's not a great rock and roll tradition to act as a backbone in Sweden, as there is in Britain or America. We feel we are battling against the Swedish styles, while we are trying to compete with what's going on world-wide.'

It is a sobering thought that Abba are the only non-British winners of the Eurovision Song Contest to ever have a second hit in Britain, and it demonstrates the reasoning behind their fear that they, like so many before them, would be left tied to the Eurovision post. Bjorn says. 'Getting rid of the Eurovision stamp has been our biggest problem. The win was a great boost to us, but we didn't want it to stay with us like an albatross. With so many previous winners of the contest, you heard the almost sneering remark: "Oh, they were the Eurovision winners," as if it were something they were tainted with. We were unknown, or virtually unknown, outside Sweden before the contest, so we were possibly more likely than many others to be labelled in that way. I'm glad to say that the hit records we have produced since "Waterloo" have somewhat smothered that memory. All round the world now, we are finding that critics and other people have stopped referring to us as "the Eurovision group". That's a great relief to us. It shows we have been truly accepted as ourselves. It is sad that so many faces have walked from the Eurovision winner's podium, only to disappear from sight – permanently – afterwards. For a while, a lot of supposedly sage and wise people were confidently predicting that the same fate was waiting for us. Deep down, I knew that it was not to happen to us, and I'm happy to know that the idea itself has now disappeared. For us, the win was not the end. It was just the end of the beginning.'

The group's reluctance to appear live on stage has in no way put them out of touch with the commercial world. Their Polish television film was shown throughout Eastern Europe, giving them in one afternoon an audience the Rolling Stones could not capture if they were to tour for the next hundred years. In one week in October 1976, they headed the singles charts in eleven countries and had a top ten place in three more. They had four number one hits in succession in England. Their album, 'Abba's Greatest Hits', was in the top five of the British charts for six months, grossing more than a million pounds. Yet everything about Abba projects what a pop group used not to stand for: conformity, efficiency, reliability, and a marked idea of how to live in the harsh world away from love songs. And their success has come without apparently breaking into a sweat. They have endured no exhausting and costly touring to promote their records; no wasted hours in airport lounges and suffocating hotel bedrooms. They have exploited television instead of being exploited by it – by giving the medium what it needs. They have supplied highly professional video films, arranged and produced by themselves, to television companies in more than twenty countries, with each film fitting perfectly with the mood of the record. Their days are spent in a nine to five routine when they are at work at Abba headquarters in Stockholm, an old house where Stikkan Andersson runs his businesses. There, they knuckle down to the serious business of record producing and manipulating a wealth of business offers and contracts. The exception is that while recording, they switch to a twelve-hour workday, stretching from 10 a.m. to 10 p.m.

Defying the long established folklore of pop singers, Abba have made sure from the start that they have controlled all their ouput one hundred per cent. Says Benny: 'The secret, if there is one, is to be completely ruthless about our own material. Stikkan presents us with the words in most cases to match the music which Bjorn and I have written. Bjorn and I provide the melodies by setting aside certain days in which we say: "We will now work hard on writing." If Stikkan, Bjorn, or I do not like one aspect of a song, it is scrapped at once. There have been many which have been thrown out half way through. After that, if it passes all the tests, it has to give me shivers down the back of my spine when I'm playing in the studio. Only then do I know we have a hit record.

I think it amounts to a combination of hard, very hard, work, team spirit, and a lot of instinct. As long as we are successful with this method, I don't think we'll be changing it. Not much point, is there, if we are on a winner already?'

All the major business arrangements are left to Stikkan, the mastermind who is often referred to as 'The fifth member of Abba' in precisely the same way that Brian Epstein was called 'The fifth Beatle'. *Billboard* magazine of America voted him Trendsetter of the Year in 1974 – and he was the only man to be given this accolade since Brian Epstein. In fact, they are the only two who have *ever* received it. Abba's affairs now take up half his time. Every morning at 6.30 a.m. he arrives at the turn-of-the-century house in the Stockholm block known as 'The singing lark'; the house he bought as his business headquarters from the proceeds of 'Waterloo'. It is set in the embassy district of Stockholm, which seems somehow fitting when you remember that Abba have been called the best ambassadors Sweden has ever had. Stikkan at work resembles a human dynamo, forever on the move, and always twitching with new ideas. Throughout each working day, he oversees the Abba enterprise, personally taking charge of their far-flung dealings, and never leaves the office before nine at night. He says: 'I find that getting in at 6.30 provides me with the perfect time to talk to our Australia contacts. I travel the world by telephone each day. But it is hard to keep up with the zones of all our markets, which are scattered all over the globe. We now sell everywhere, with the exception of China, North Korea, and Vietnam.'

Despite the fact that Abba rarely show their faces in public outside their promotional films, they are outselling Elton John, Rod Stewart, and the Bay City Rollers. They are a closely-knit bunch who are likely to stay together long enough to outstrip the record success in disc sales of the only group they have not yet overhauled – The Beatles. They are a talented bunch, who are also cool, calm, collected, and very calculating, in the nicest possible way. Bjorn put their feelings about tours into perspective when he says: 'We want to wait until the audiences howl for Abba to come to them. That is why we haven't yet attempted a tour of America. We want them to come to us, to ask for us, then we can do it on our terms. Besides, we don't need to tour if we don't need the money. And, if you don't need the money, the joy of hopping from hotel to hotel and living on the move surrounded by suitcases totally escapes me.'

Stikkan Andersson has his own philosophy about touring. He says: 'The tour in February is to be our first of Britain, and other people in the music business have been saying: "How on earth can you make it in a big way without the help of television or touring?" I tell them we are doing it the opposite way, and we have proven it can be done. I am also aware that we could over-expose ourselves, and what would be the point of that, especially as we don't have to make frequent appearances? I don't want television to use us. I want us to use television. Take England, for example, where we have not had any television shows of our own and have avoided touring as yet. What we have done there is make appearances on Top of the Pops a few times a year. I think that is enough. I have seen exactly the opposite position arise in Australia, where I feel we have been ever-exposed on television. Despite this, we are still in very good shape in Australia because they have really taken us to their hearts. The over-exposure as far as television there is concerned came about, not through our design, but by the chance that the Australian television companies went round the world buying up television shows of us which had been made in countries like Germany and France. I have put a stop to that sort of thing now. If we make a programme in a particular country, I make sure there is a clause in the contract which restricts its use to that country. That way, we can avoid the saturation coverage which can only do us harm in the long run.

'Tours of America are very much on our mind, and we could take up offers tomorrow if we were so inclined. But now is not the time. I am sure of that. I don't feel we should do tours there until we are as big in the United States as we are in Europe and Australia. When that moment arrives, as I'm sure it will, then we will go there. I know there are some people in the States who are laughing at our attitude, saying we think we are God or something. We don't. We have our feet firmly on the ground. The refusal isn't out of arrogance on our part. We just want to make sure we attack what is, after all, the biggest market in the world, in exactly the right way.

'A lot of groups and other musicians or singers do spend most of their time working in America. It is possible that at some time in the future, Abba will be bidding for a share of the American concert circuit, in our own way and our own time. The reaction of some of the "experts" there is: "But how will you become big enough if you don't tour?" They haven't read the situation as well as I have. Look at it this way: we can go to the United States, say, twice a year for television promotion, when we are seen by millions rather than the thousands who attend concerts. When those millions who have seen our promotions want us to go over, that's our moment. It's the way we have handled it in every other country. We have waited until Abba have become big names in a particular country before we have visited to tour, and we have managed it slowly but surely. Remember The Beatles waited until they had big selling records in America before they went on tour there. And look what was waiting for them. That phenomenal reception at New York, the like of which had not been seen anywhere in the world. They never looked back.

'I patiently waited for just the right moment in Holland, Germany, Norway, France, England, and so on – and I am patiently waiting for the same moment to announce itself in America. And we can afford to wait. We are doing well enough elsewhere for the moment, thank you. Of course, I do realise that there is the risk we will never happen in a big way in America if we don't tour there, but that is a risk I am prepared to take. The rest of the world is not so small, not for us. I think the Americans will take to us, and I think we'll see a reaction to Abba similar to the one we got from Australians and Europeans.

'I just got a call from Oslo, where the seven thousand seats on offer for a concert went in three hours. And Gothenberg, where nine thousand tickets sold out in just over two hours. That's never happened before, not even with acts like Liza Minnelli or the Rolling Stones. All our dates in Europe are sell-outs, and we are very excited, and looking forward to the tour both there and in Australia. But we realise the tour must be for a limited time only. For, apart from all the other considerations, we can't spend a lot of time touring because we need that time to work on our records. It takes us such a long time to write and produce an LP. Our latest, "Arrival", for example, took us eighteen months. I'm not saying we were working on it all the time, but it was spread over that period because of all the interruptions. We'll be giving ourselves just a week's rest here in Sweden at the end of the European part of our tour. Then we go down to Australia for fourteen days, taking in Sydney, Brisbane, Adelaide, and Perth. But we haven't been able to keep everybody happy there, much as we would like to. There have been complaints because, unfortunately, we will not be able to get to Queensland at all. Even the Prime Minister of Queensland cabled, asking us to go there, but we had to reply: "Sorry, we can't." I hope I have been able to explain it adequately to them. Once again, it is a matter of too little time for us.

'When we finish in Australia in mid-March, we'll be flying back home again and from April up to probably October we'll be working on our next LP. All that time we'll not be doing anything else. For us, it will be undiluted concentration on producing and writing. This is the only chance we have to survive. Songs don't come to us in an afternoon. We have to polish them, work on them till they are exactly right for us. If we don't hide away and work like that, in an intently concentrated way, there will be no new Abba LP. We have no choice. Then we have promised to go to the United States and South America for television and promotion. If we start to click in the States, we'll be able to think in terms of a tour there in the spring or summer of 1978. I think that possibility is in the balance, but we couldn't do anything before then.

'Our position is that promoters are already asking us for more time than we have available. It's very hard to explain to them why we are turning down touring work, and they don't seem to understand. I have to explain what it all depends on, and that we can't tour all the time because we need the time to slip away for every moment we can squeeze out to write our music and songs. Some of them shrug their shoulders, and think I'm a little crazy, but I know I'm not.'

Each member of the group has a personal and individual feeling about tours. For Agnetha, they are painful, because she hates leaving her young daughter, Linda, behind. She said: 'Before Brighton the only times I had to be away from Linda was when we were doing the studio work. That meant going just a few miles, and being away for just a few hours. Touring is a different matter. Don't get me wrong. I am as excited as anybody about what has happened to us, but for me there is a tinge of sadness when I think of Linda. I miss her so much. I like to be with her as much as I can, so I go on the tours with a mixture of emotions. When I am at home, I spend all my time with Linda, and we have such a lot of fun. When it comes time to go off, I find going away so very difficult, but we are fortunate in having a nanny who looks after her well.'

It is the thought of Linda at home which makes Bjorn and Agnetha homesick on their travels. Wherever they are in the world, they make long and expensive telephone calls to keep in touch with her. 'It's funny that she has got used to us going off and coming on the telephone later to talk to her,' said Agnetha. 'Of course, she can't imagine how far we are away.'

Benny has his own special memories of the tours. The food. 'Eating is the only fun thing when you're on tour,' he said. 'You go from one hotel to another, from one town to another, and from one country to another – and the only thing you remember afterwards is what you've eaten at the different stops. In fact, I think that is the one department where we have been spoiled. Some years ago, we'd be happy to grab a cheese sandwich for supper in a motel when we were touring the *folkparks*. Now it's champagne and lobsters and caviare, and I'm not complaining. But there is one thing I've noticed, which seems very unfair to me. When Bjorn and I eat a lot, we get fat. When Agnetha and Anni-Frid eat a lot, they stay exactly as they are. How is that? They've obviously got a secret we don't know anything about.'

When Abba visited Germany, the promoters of the tour were astonished to find that the back-up team of technicians stayed in the same Hilton Hotels that the group went to. Astonished, because previously they had noticed that while English groups stayed in all the best hotels, their 'fringe' members were despatched across town to lesser hotels. Said Benny: 'I'm surprised that that is a surprise to them. Why shouldn't they stay where we stay? They are on the tour because they can do a fine job for us, and because we need them. So what sort of people would we be if we sent them off to hotels where we didn't really want to stay? That sort of thing smacks of almost class prejudice, and I don't think you'll find us getting into that. It's not our way, and it's not the Swedish way. To some people it may seem a bit of extravagance, but to us it just makes sense. We are aware that we have risen to the crest of the wave because of team effort, and we want to make sure that every member of that team is treated equally. I think that, because of that attitude, we get a lot in return from the people we work with. It is also the reason we have a smooth running operation, without hang-ups and dissension. I know it may sound corny to say we have a big, happy family, but that's exactly how it is.'

The legendary generosity of Abba showed itself in Australia, where the group bought £15,000 worth of exotic clothes for their appearance on the television special – and afterwards gave the lot away to their fans.

Abba are like California wine, which has no vintage years because every year is one. The sun of the aptly dubbed Sunshine

State beams down on the growing vines with unfailing regularity, ripening the grapes to perfection. Each Abba record has a similar experience. They all find No 1 slots with a similar, unfailing regularity.

When the group topped both the single and LP charts of the *New Musical Express* in Britain for 1976 it was just another milestone on the way. Topping charts with singles and albums, an unfulfilled dream of so many performers, has become for Abba a commonplace experience.

Not that they are, or probably ever will be, nonchalant or bored with their seemingly guaranteed accolades.

Every time a new record is released, Bjorn goes through the agony of tension which has been with him since he made his first faltering steps into show business. He will never change. It is part of his makeup and his nature.

'I suppose that, deep down, all of us realise that it's got to end somewhere,' said Bjorn.

'Each time we release a new Abba record I wonder "Is this it? Is this the last big one?" Or, worse still, "Is this the record that is going to disappear without trace and tell us it is time to get out of the business?"

'If we turned out a record which we really believed in and saw it make no impact on the charts, that would scare all of us. I know I'm supposed to be the nervy one, but at that moment my friends would react exactly as I would.'

Bjorn's apparent shakiness has never affected the so-far inevitable result of a new Abba release and the group has still not put a foot wrong. They have seen seven consecutive singles soar to the top of the charts in Britain and at one moment recently they had three LPs in the top 30. World sales have roared past 60 million and reached such a frenetic pace – selling at a faster rate than the Beatles ever did – that Abba is now a bigger export earner for Sweden than the famous and globally revered Volvo cars.

Said Bjorn, 'I'm sure it must seem strange, but with all this success around us, which everybody else assumes is inevitable, I can't help wondering when the bubble will burst.'

Despite Bjorn's cautiousness, the Abba bandwagon shows no signs of slowing down. 'Abba – The Album' and their single 'Take a Chance on Me' both rocketed to take a firm hold on the No 1 spots in Britain simultaneously and with breathtaking speed.

And the long awaited No 1 in the United States of America happened with 'Dancing Queen', after hovering around just below for a short while. That was the realisation of a dream for Abba, who know the American market is the only major one which has not succumbed to their embrace of success. The members of the group and Stikkan Andersson are multi-millionaires already and don't need the money they could earn in America, but cracking the market there has become a matter of pride for the cool Swedes.

'I'm certain it is only a matter of a very short time before we make it as big over there as we have in Britain, all over Europe, and Australia,' said Stikkan Andersson. 'The groundwork with our associates there has been carried out very carefully and when the time is right we will move.'

Their 'Arrival' album sold 739,000 records and cassettes in Sweden in a year – a fabulous achievement in a country with a population of just over eight million. They followed this with the meteoric single, 'Name of the Game', which sold 140,000 in advance order Swedish copies even before it was issued.

The rat-tat-tat of unfailing success had little or no effect on the rigidly highbrow press of Sweden. The knockers were there in force to disdainfully play down the group's achievements and transparently obvious public appeal. *Expressen*, the Stockholm daily which leads the sales league, had half a word of praise for 'Arrival'. Their critic judged that the record was 'strong and professional'. But he condemned the effort by describing the lyrics as 'common . . . and very bad'.

Perhaps it is the effect of this type of home grown criticism which gives Bjorn his outlook on life.

He said, 'Yes, I am weary of the so-called experts panning us like this all the time. If our future had been decided by the judgement of "experts" we would not have one.

'They have a right to their own opinion, of course. But I can't help noticing that their opinions are not reflected by the millions of people all over the world who regularly buy our records and battle over tickets for our concerts.'

Savage critics or no, Abba are regularly accorded the sincerest form of flattery – imitation. Other groups and singers have joined in the Abba stampede to record their songs. There are 544 different versions of their songs, which have been made in 24 countries. Top of this particular league is 'Waterloo', which so far can claim 92 versions.

There is no need for Abba to cock a snook at the home critics. The phenomena of their worldwide success speaks for itself. In their first four years at the top, their gross earnings have topped £250 million, and the astute stewardship of Stikkan Andersson has ensured that the earnings accrue to Abba's company instead of to an army of hangers-on of the type just about every other recording artiste has had to carry.

'The achievements of Abba are there for all to see,' said Stikkan Andersson. 'The critics can make what they like of them and say what they like, but they can't take anything away from Abba's unique position in the world of music.'

No lack of confidence is apparent in the bold running of Polar Music and the orchestration of Abba's career. When Stikkan Andersson planned the Christmas 1977 LP, 'Abba – The Album' – rated as their best ever – orders went in for a million records and cassettes for the Swedish market alone. Plants in Tel Aviv, Paris, and Vienna were alerted in case they had to be called on to help meet the demand.

The reluctance of Sweden's establishment to recognise the phenomena in their midst was clearly demonstrated by the state run television corporation. Not until late in 1976 did they deign to accord Abba a show. It was an hour long documentary of Abba at work and at play but could only be found air time on the number two channel and was put together on an ultra-low budget. It was a belated recognition, but very much a begrudging kind. Still, the programme delighted the mass of Swedish fans who, for the first time, could sit at home and watch Abba singing and giving long interviews on television.

There has been no such reluctance in a very unexpected area, the Iron Curtain countries of Eastern Europe. The Polish state television invited Abba over to appear and, in a very capitalistic manner, provided a charter aircraft to fly the group and their team to Warsaw.

The Abba financial mandarins also dreamed up a remarkable arrangement whereby the group could sell their records to Iron Curtain countries and receive the money in Sweden, circumventing the strict currency control regulations of Communist countries. This called for a barter system, whereby the royalties over and above the allowed quota are paid in oil, which is then sold and converted to cash.

Said Benny, 'I am reliably informed that our method of getting oil is very much easier than drilling for it.'

In Russia, Abba LP's, limited by the financial quotas, change hands on a flourishing black market for £125 each.

'It's heartbreaking to see people having to do this, but laws are laws and the quota restrictions make this happen,' said Bjorn. 'We'd like to see a flood of our records putting selling of this kind out of court and the black marketeers put out of business, but that's not possible because it's just not allowed.'

Early in 1977 Abba set off on their first world tour, which took them to Britain for their first live concerts, all over Europe, and to the country which has taken the foursome to its heart more than any other, Australia.

First stops involved hops around Scandinavia. Even the fans there greet Abba with a pulsating excitement which belies their more familiar Nordic reserve. The demand for seats was so fierce that touts were able to realise £100 each for tickets outside the Scandinavium, a giant hockey stadium in Gothenberg.

On the European section of the tour alone, taking in Sweden, Denmark, Norway, West Germany, Holland, and Britain, their concerts were seen by 90,000 people, who paid a total of half a million pounds for the privilege. It was a triumphant, almost regal procession. But the profits left for Abba did not amount to very much in the end. Most of the gate money went in paying the salaries and travelling expenses of the fifty-two entourage members, musicians and roadies who travelled with them, and for the transport of their thirty tons of equipment in a fleet of four trucks.

The concerts contained a new innovation and a preview peek into Abba's future. With every single and album they turned out making an unimpeded dash to the top of the charts, Abba were keen to try something more adventurous. So they wrote their own pop opera. It was a fairly light-hearted story of a beautiful Swedish girl who left her home and friends to become a superstar. That part of the story bore a certain resemblance to the true lives of Agnetha and Anni-Frid. The rest strode into the realm of pure fiction. In the opera story, fame only brought the girl loneliness and misery in its wake. And that in no way mirrors the experience of the two Abba girls. Agnetha and Anni-Frid both wore identical wigs and outfits for the opera so that it was impossible for the audience to tell them apart.

Though the opera was certainly not gloomy it did represent a serious step for the group. It was their first attempt to actually say something a little meaningful through their songs. Not that they were trying to build a foundation of 'serious message' music. That has never been Abba's intent or purpose, and probably never will be. Bjorn has always said, 'Our music is designed to entertain and give people pleasure. That's all. There is no political motivation behind it, and we're not aiming to change the world.'

Their songs have always been jolly, and the words have been intentionally light.

Abba maintained their top of the pops magic in the show with offerings of 'Waterloo', 'Ring Ring', 'I Do, I Do', 'Mamma Mia', 'Fernando', 'Dancing Queen', 'S.O.S.', 'Honey, Honey', and 'Money, Money, Money'. That pleased the fans, but as John Blake, popexpert and Ad Lib columnist for the *London Evening News*, wrote, 'With Anna and Frida looking as they do I, for one, would be happy even if they didn't sing a note.'

Abbamania hit Britain when the group swept in to tackle

appearances in Birmingham, Manchester, Glasgow, and two final blockbuster shows at London's Albert Hall, the concert venue built on the orders of Queen Victoria in memory of her dead husband, Prince Albert, and known intimately to the world's greatest musicians and the royalty of show business.

The four members of Abba spent months rehearsing their show to make sure it was worth all the ballyhoo which preceded it and that their fans were not let down in grabbing the rare opportunity of seeing them in the flesh.

'We did not want to put a toe wrong,' said Bjorn. 'Tours of this kind take so long to prepare for and mount that it would be silly to have them go off at anything but the highest pitch of perfection. They are the only occasions the fans can see us on stage, so we have to make sure everything is just right.

'To make sure the shows on the tour went over as we wanted them to, we worked and worked at rehearsals in Stockholm over a period of literally months. It was a very, very tiring time, but it was all worth the effort in the end. The ecstatic reaction of the audiences to us on the tour was all the reward we wanted, and that made all the effort worthwhile.

'A very special moment for us was at the Albert Hall in London, where the thousands of fans packed in displayed their enjoyment so much. They showed how much they liked our music, and that's always great news for artistes. I'll never forget their reaction when we sang "Fernando" and they all joined in to sing along with us. It was electric, vibrant.

'For me it was a milestone in Abba's career. I never thought I would see it happen, but years ago it was the sort of thing I would imagine in my most far-fetched dreams.'

Said Benny, 'I remember a moment in the middle of the Albert Hall night when I thought, "Good grief, Benny, this is you sitting here playing at the Albert Hall." I felt completely overawed for a few seconds. For a little while I could not believe it was me there. And, believe me, it was very hard for me to sit steady on my stool. That feeling passed, but it was all something that totally overwhelmed me, and it's a night I will never forget, no matter how long I live.'

More than a million people sent in postal applications for the 12,000 tickets for the group's two concerts at the Albert Hall. £6 tickets were selling on the black market, with no shortage of takers, for as much as £50 each. Abba would have had to hold a hundred concerts at the Hall to accommodate all the fans who wanted to see them.

Whenever the group stepped out of their heavily guarded hotels, they were mobbed by members of the public eager to enjoy a rare close look at them or to collect their autographs. But columnist John Blake noticed that they seemed to have frozen in their dealings with the press. In his Ad Lib column he wrote, 'Abba appear to have turned into the most uncommunicative bunch of Swedes since Greta Garbo. During their brief visit to Britain the group refused to appear on TV or radio and refused to give newspaper or magazine interviews . . . But I still feel the group were going a bit far by forcing myself and other critics to stand at the back of theatres.'

Their appearance at the Odeon, Birmingham, on the first stop of their British tour, gave them a glimpse of the virulent local politics. The three thousand audience was searched as it filed into the auditorium, which is just minutes from the two Birmingham city centre pubs, the Mulberry Bush and the Tavern in the Town, which were blitzed just over two years before when dozens of young people were killed in the worst ever IRA bomb atrocity. Police, fearing a new IRA action in the packed Odeon, took no chances.

Concert dates throughout the tour were booked out months ahead, in places as diverse as Manchester, Copenhagen, and Perth, Australia. The tickets for the two Perth concerts were sold as soon as they went on offer. 42,000 orders for the 16,000 tickets were received on the day the box office opened.

The threat of bombings followed them across the world to Perth when a telephone call warned that a bomb would explode during the show, killing Abba. The 8,000 audience had to file out of the concert hall while an army of police moved in to search for the bomb. Twenty minutes later police gave the 'all clear' and Abba went back on stage to complete their show.

Benny Andersson was as nervous a performer as he had been at the Albert Hall, but for a very different reason. For, during the police search of the auditorium, he had remained a lone figure on stage. Nobody had told him about the bomb threat. He said, 'When I discovered what had been going on my legs felt like jelly. Everybody else knew, and I wanted to know why no-one had told me about it. Why, I might have been blown to bits.'

For the Australian tour Abba hired a Boeing 727 to transport them and the 117 people working with them. 17 of these were Australian musicians who played in only two of their songs. All a sign of the attention to detail and perfectionist attitude which is so much part of Abba and their work.

A violent rainstorm greeted their first Australian concert, which, unfortunately for them and the audience, took place in an open air arena. The 20,000 audience didn't mind getting wet and wanted to stay in their seats no matter how wet they got, so the Abba show went on. But it was difficult with puddles and a screen of water all over the stage. A team of stagehands tried to soak up the water, but it was a losing battle. Everybody had difficulty in keeping on their feet and poor Anni-Frid, doing her gyrating as she sang, came a cropper and dented her elegant bottom when she slipped and made a most ungracious fall. The others leaped to her aid but, luckily, she did not hurt herself. And, at the end, the foursome got a very special roar of appreciation from the audience.

Said Anni-Frid later, 'The rainstorm came out of nowhere. But the audience were clearly going to stay whatever the weather to see us. So, in those circumstances, we were definitely going ahead with our show. The tumble shook me up, but that's all. It was a small price to pay when the fans were showing such great loyalty.'

A shade of Aussie politics later intruded on their progress of adulation across the island continent. The recently installed Prime Minister, Malcolm Fraser, wanted the group to appear in Canberra, the country's capital, and seat and home of the national politicians. Abba manager Stikkan Andersson explained that this had not been planned in the tour and was not possible. So Fraser tried to entice the group to his 'home town' by offering to fly them there in a government plane. Stikkan was unmoved. Local taxpayers were not. They were the ones who would have had to foot the bill, and they considered it an outrageous move on the part of Fraser, whose government was in the middle of a very stringent austerity programme, exhorting the population to all sorts of belt-tightening. Fraser had to display some nimble footwork to avoid a political storm. And Abba, who like to keep clear of any controversy of this type, were relieved that none of the bricks flying around hit them.

A bigger innovation was just round the corner for Abba. Their first film.

A very bright idea, really. For, if making personal appearances is so difficult and expensive for them, why not substitute a film appearance for a lot of arduous touring? And they can reach even more fans via the screen than on tour.

Said Benny, 'You can say that the film will take the place of our 1978 concert tour. Now we can stay at home for a year and not feel guilty.'

Abba used their Australian connection to set the film up. During the 1977 tour there, the leading Swedish film director Lasse Hallstrom was called out to make 'Abba – The Movie'. Tied in with their new LP release, 'Abba – The Album', – which also claimed an Australian flavour – it was a perfectly orchestrated and dovetailed marketing operation.

The storyline of the film is simplicity itself. A disc jockey called Ashley is assigned to follow the group around on the sell-out tour of Australia. Ashley hopes to get an 'exclusive gut-level dialogue' with Abba for his radio station, but the likeable, inexperienced fellow is hopelessly out of his depth. In vain, he chases them from Sydney to Perth, then to Adelaide, before accidentally running into them in Melbourne. He turns up at the wrong places and is usually one jet flight behind the group. He even misses the press conference where Agnetha, the group's wiggling blonde, is asked to confirm whether she has the sexiest bottom and replies demurely, 'How do I know? I've never seen it.'

For his troubles, Ashley is repeatedly thrown out of concert halls and dressing rooms. But the movie provides a happy ending for him when he gets the interview he has sought so relentlessly.

The film is strictly a vehicle for Abba to sing 26 of their top songs in fine open air surroundings, and the storyline is designed merely to provide short breathing spaces between them.

An army of film businessmen from all over the world turned up for a special preview of 'Abba – The Movie' in Stockholm. They saw it for what it is, a carrier for Abba songs and presentation and, they correctly judged, exactly what the fans wanted. Warner Brothers won the right to world distribution of the film by bidding a small fortune for it.

'Abba – The Movie' exploded onto the public with its world premiere in Sydney, Australia, on 15th December, 1977, to a packed house of screaming fans. The chosen venue was a salute to Aussie Abbamania, a disease the country has contracted and shows no signs of recovering from.

The four members of Abba attended the London premiere at the Warner Theatre in Leicester Square in February, 1978, which coincided with the week their single, 'Take a Chance on Me', was in the No 1 spot.

Said Benny, 'We are always delighted to come to Britain. After all, it was here that we won the Eurovision Song Contest, and that's something we'll always remember as the biggest milestone in our career.'

British critics have always been generous to Abba, and this occasion was not to prove any different. Arthur Thirkell, film critic of the *Daily Mirror*, wrote, 'Now the fans can enjoy the sight as well as the sound of the wholesome Swedes ... It's a film that is as pure as freshly churned butter.' And, underlining Abba's special position in an era which is finding itself dominated by the onslaught of punk rock, Cecil Wilson of the *Daily Mail* wrote, 'One good reason for devoting a whole 95-

minute film to these Swedish idols is that they project a wholesome, natural vitality and look as if they wash. Another is that they sing better music than most of their British rivals and also, whenever their shrill electronic accompaniment allows us to hear the words, better English.'

Thomson Prentice, show business writer for the *Daily Mail*, saw clearly the reasoning behind the exercise. He wrote, 'With stunning simplicity, they have created a screen image of themselves which provides a substitute for personal appearances.'

The mass ecstasy of the fans displayed so well in the film, which is really a documentary of their Australian tour, was not repeated when the film had its Swedish premiere in Stockholm at Christmas, 1977. There were no mob scenes. For, after all, isn't imagining a Swedish mob like visualising Bjorn Borg getting rattled in a tennis match?

In stark contrast to reviewers all over the rest of the world, the Swedish critics, with one lone exception, refused to warm to the film. The *Expressen* reviewer said he considered it a fine film. But the other papers followed their familiar anti-Abba route and panned it.

This, of course, in no way affected the film's popularity with the public. It was shown all over Sweden and was as big a success there as anywhere else.

A few days before the film was unleashed, Agentha was to experience an even bigger moment in her life. The birth of her second child, an 8-lbs 5-oz boy, Peter Christian. Agnetha had worked through the first six months of her pregnancy, keeping up a strenuous round of recording and preparations for the film. Then she confined herself to her home to await the birth.

But she was determined that the birth of Peter, in a hospital near Stockholm, should not be turned into a public circus. Over the official Swedish news agency, it was announced that there would be no press conference and that only one photographer of Abba's choice would be allowed to take pictures. And afterwards only a single picture of Agnetha and the baby would be issued to the world's press.

This was Abba pulling the weight that their exalted position in the world of pop allows. There was a time in the early days of their career when they were glad to talk to anybody and gather any publicity that was available and on offer to them. Now they are noticeably cooler, and control their exposure with a very firm hand. They are very aware that their success allows them to call the shots to suit themselves. This attitude has angered a number of journalists. Others see it more philosophically as the natural course of events.

Shortly after the birth, Agnetha issued a special appeal to the fans to keep away from their home because she wanted plenty of peace and quiet for the baby. The kids responded and the Ulvaeus household enjoyed an air of tranquillity for a while.

This second child was to mark a change in Agnetha's life. From Peter's birth, she was to spend less time working with Abba. She still recorded with them, of course, but whenever possible she would duck out of what was going on and get home to Peter and her now five-year-old daughter, Linda. Skeletal plans for the long-awaited America tour were scrapped because Agnetha did not want to be forced to spend months away from her baby. And when Abba were needed abroad for promotion in connection with records or, particularly, with their film, Agnetha stayed behind in Stockholm till the last minute. The others might be away for a few days but Agnetha would fly in on the day of an appearance, stay a few hours for it, then head back.

'It's all a question of priorities,' said Agnetha. 'Of course Abba is very important to me, but the most important people in my life are my family.'

There were rumours that the new baby would spell the end of any Abba tours. It was clear that Agnetha would be quite happy if she never stepped on stage again. And it is no secret that Abba have now earned so much money that they are under no pressures or obligations to do anything other than just what they want.

Agnetha refutes such stories.

'I just want to be sure that I spend all of Peter's first

months with him,' she said. 'I want to see every second of his babyhood. There's no reason why I should cheat myself out of that, is there? After all, it is something that all mothers take for granted. But after that period it'll be back to normal. Although if a conflict of interest arises between Abba and my children, it will be no contest. My children will always win.'

The biggest question facing Abba now is: Where do we go from here? There is so much interest and controversy about this question that a different rumour goes round the pop fraternity in Stockholm almost every week. One will have them giving up the tours completely. Another going to live abroad. Another retiring from show business completely. There seems no end to the rumours, and to their diversity.

Fuelling the rumours are statements like a recent one from Anni-Frid when she said, 'What we used to dream about doesn't seem so important now. Our success doesn't seem to be so important.' For when people do get tired of success, they really are thinking of cashing in their chips and going home. And remember that Anni-Frid is the girl whose life has been motivated since many years back by an overwhelming desire to find success.

Even Bjorn has helped the stories along by saying, 'I was much happier ten years ago before all this started. All this travelling has given me a pain in my stomach which I've had for the past six months.'

A chink in the happy-go-lucky façade of Benny appeared when he told a Norwegian newspaper, 'I think we can see the beginning of the end of the Abba saga. Abba will exist as long as we enjoy it, but no longer.'

Bjorn asserts, 'Don't get us wrong about this. Abba has been the centre of our lives and I think we'll be together for a long time yet. But I can't bear the thought of us being Abba and fifty at the same time. Ugh! What a thought. By then, we will have long moved on to something else.

'I am aware that people remember how the Beatles broke up in a glare of publicity and with a lot of bad feeling around. They are wondering if that will happen to us. I can answer that question right now. We will not go in that way. We will stay together as Abba for as long as it continues to be fun and what we want.

'One thing in our favour is that we are two pairs rather than four individuals. We were friends before we thought of forming a group. And our private lives are very important to us, which is why we keep them private.

'We will never split because of the strain of travelling and working together. Peering into the future, I feel that one day we will split up because it suits us all. We all had individual careers before, and we could all switch to working solo if we wanted to. It's not a moment I hold any fears for.'

Benny agrees. 'I think one day we'll just decide to stop working together without in any way being angry with each other,' he said.

Abba are still sitting firmly on the crest of the wave of unparalleled success. But the cool Swedish millionaires are astute enough to be planning what they will do when the bubble bursts, as it inevitably must one day.

Anni-Frid takes solo singing and dancing lessons every day and also fits in a strict keep-fit regime.

'I did very well as a solo singer before Abba, and I'd have no qualms about working on my own again,' she said. 'Although that seems a long way off in the future, I am aware it is an eventuality I must be prepared for.'

Said Agnetha, 'If Abba went the way of so many other groups, I'd possibly become a full time mother. Or, if I wanted to stay in show business, I would probably concentrate on acting. I did a bit before, and also in the making of our film. I enjoyed it very much, I must say, and I'd like the chance to cultivate it.'

Bjorn and Benny have been very successful as songwriters and it is in that direction that they would be inclined to concentrate their talents.

Said Bjorn, 'Along with Stikkan, Benny and I have written all of Abba's songs and we know there's a lot of steam left in us yet. But there's no way we would switch to full time song-writing while Abba still exists. For the next few years at least you can be assured the group will be what gets all our energies.'

The most persistent rumour which repeatedly circulates around the foursome is that they are weary of the confiscatory Swedish taxes and plan to move abroad as tax exiles.

All four refute this notion.

Said Bjorn, 'Swedish taxes are high, but it's not as if we have any financial worries. And we don't even have expensive tastes. We have houses, summer cottages and small boats, and we have discovered that we don't need much more.'

Conversely, a surfeit of wealth recently proved a problem for Bjorn and Agnetha when they decided to move house. Their old home was so valuable they could not find anybody to buy it, and eventually settled for leaving it to the Norwegian Embassy.

'No, we will never leave Sweden,' asserts Bjorn. 'This is our home, we love it, and where would we go?'

The others feel exactly the same because Sweden offers what nowhere else can. The opportunity to live as private people. In Stockholm, they are not mobbed in the street and can move about freely. Benny and Anni-Frid love to go to the theatre, and regularly visit theatres all over town. A few people may point them out to friends, but that is all.

'I know from the experience of others and from our overseas visits that we could not live abroad with the peace and freedom that we enjoy here,' said Benny. 'We're very grateful for that, and it's something we are not going to give up.'

Because of the heavy work load that Abba had to shoulder in 1977, they decided to slow down the following year. But only as Abba. As the business heads of Polar Music along with Stikkan Andersson, Bjorn and Benny worked as hard as ever. They opened a new art gallery in Stockholm called A. H. Graphic. As further diversification in business, they announced plans for the building of a million pound recording studio in the centre of Stockholm. And they gained reassurance, if they needed any, from a financial report which rated Abba's company as the most successful in Sweden.

But the Abba dream which has taken Bjorn, Benny, Anni-Frid and Agnetha so far will take a long time to die. They recently expressed interest in doing a musical together. Not a mini-opera like the one on their tour, but a full-blown musical which would be good enough to stage on New York's Broadway. They imagine seeing their lights above the theatre, sitting in a place of glory on Broadway's Great White Way.

After the heady success of the past few years, could they still be just four stage-struck kids at heart?

CHAPTER FIFTEEN

# BUT NO SWEDISH RHAPSODY

The world acclaim of Abba has hardly caused a ripple on the surface of the traditional Swedish stoic reserve. The global reputation of the group is as high as Swedish steel or Volvo cars, but at home they have become the whipping boy for critics seeking to lambast 'commercial' music and promote songs carrying lyrics promoting social awareness. The fans were delighted after Brighton, but the rest of Sweden could manage only a long and luxurious yawn. That attitude has still not changed. Though over half a million copies of the 'Arrival' album were sold in Sweden in the space of three weeks, they are still looked on as just another Swedish group; people don't seem able to see the measure of their international success. As popular as Abba have become in England, Australia, all over Europe and elsewhere, they are not, and perhaps never will be, accorded their proper recognition at home. Swedes still cling to the belief that that sort of thing can't happen to a Swedish group. Even though it has.

Ingmar Bergmann, the legendary film director, was a victim of exactly the same narrow Swedish vision. The apparently myopic Swedes did not realise what a genius they had in their midst and, though he wanted to stay, he was eventually driven out, helped on his way by some heavy-handed tactics from the tax authorities. They had the same attitude to Dag Hammarskjold, the Swedish statesman who became Secretary-General of the United Nations and built up the prestige of the international organisation until his death in a plane crash in the Congo in 1961. His appointment was a great honour for Sweden, but few people there seemed to appreciate it.

A rival Swedish record producer offered the opinion: 'If Abba broke all the record records all over the world, the Swedes would say: "But they are only a Swedish group." We are a strange people. We love everything from abroad, but we tend to denigrate anything that is Swedish. We don't think anything from here can amount to a hill of beans in the international reckoning, which is nonsense, of course. But that's the way of things here. It's a national characteristic, I'm afraid. We don't realise what an impact they have made, and I don't think the everyday person ever will. The music business is, not unnaturally, the single exception. We could see what was happening with the miracle of Abba, and in the Swedish pop world, they are referred to, somewhat reverently, as The Group. Because as far as the business here is concerned, Abba is THE GROUP. But as soon as you step outside those narrow confines, the story is very different. Stikkan Andersson was forever talking about his protégés as being the greatest, the biggest, the best. People didn't take much notice when Stikkan announced that Abba were going to take the pop world by storm. Their reaction was: "Stikkan is always beating a big drum. It doesn't mean much." He was like the little boy who cried wolf so many times to gain attention. When the real thing came along, no-one took any notice. They were right about Stikkan beating the publicity tom-tom very loud; he is, in fact, a very gifted publicist. But they were wrong about Abba. They were something different, something special. The evidence was there for all to hear, and anyone who took the trouble to listen would have spotted their class and style, which is unmistakable. Even with their records riding high in the charts of countries in every part of the world, it still does not get home, and I get the feeling that it never will.'

After Brighton, the only offer from Swedish television for an Abba appearance came from a cosy, sit-down talk programme for elderly folk. The group would have accepted even this, but had to turn it down when they were told they would have to work with the studio band. They said they could only appear with their own musicians, or not at all. Said Bjorn: 'This was only fair, because the Abba sound is produced accurately only when we have our own people working with us. To try it any other way would cheat the public – and us – out of what is expected.'

The group also pointed out that every television station in the world allows artistes to work to their own music, but the intransigence of Swedish television kept them off the screens. Over the years, Abba have been asked repeatedly why they don't do television in Sweden, and their reply has been: 'Nobody ever asks us.' In fact, their first appearance on Swedish television following the Eurovision win was in January, 1975 – and then they only got on a programme because another Swedish group was forced to cry off when their lead singer caught a cold.

The connection with the Abba herring concern was raised by Mia Gerdis of *Dagens Nyheters*, who wrote: 'It's said that Abba is dead as a herring. I saw that they moved and I heard that they sang, but they couldn't give me the impression of being alive.'

Her colleague, Anders Klintevall, also of *Dagens Nyheters*, was equally scathing: 'Their music is just good to dance to. That's all. Four beats in a bar. It's the "Ring, Ring" and "Waterloo" mixture again. This boom-boom-boom like a machine, for me, is a sign of cynicism and poor music talent. They use the same formula again and again, as if they are trying to wear it out. As long as it is "what the people want" it will be repeated until it *is* worn out. I was bored by them.'

Another typical review of Abba came from Mats Olsson, pop columnist of *Expressen*. 'Their music is tough and professional, but the lyrics are deplorable . . . They sound like the result of a meeting between 10 c.c. and the Beach Boys in a discotheque. Their production is good, but the technique and effects make the music seem cold. Another strike against them is their lyrics, which are empty of feelings and ideas. I haven't anything against so-called "love lyrics" but they should be real. The listener should be able to believe them, and even feel them. Is Stikkan Andersson guilty of the worst lyrics? It seems so, because when Bjorn and Benny are the sole composers, the lyrics are that tiny bit better. But they are still not good. Don't Abba have any feelings of their own? Don't they have opinions on the world around them?' Olsson followed this up with a review of the 'Abba' album, when he conceded: 'There is no really bad tune on this record,' but added: 'Though it is easy for them to write songs that you remember, there are no messages. But they don't claim to have a message.'

'Yes, that is so – we don't claim we are trying to put over a message,' retorts Bjorn. 'What we are doing is trying to write and present songs which people can enjoy. We have no illusions about our music changing the world. We are entertainers, pure and simple. The messages we leave to those more qualified than us to deliver them.'

In fact, Abba are concerned about the carping reviews they get in the Swedish press. They take their music seriously. But they point to their continuing success as their defence and their judge. They find they can't do much about the prevailing views of pop writers in Sweden, whose task seems to be to chastise the commercialism of music. They somehow expect the artistes to concentrate their music on socialistic ideals.

Yet another *Dagens Nyheters* critic, Silvert Bramstedt, found such a platform from which to attack the recent release of the album, 'Arrival'. He said: 'Abba is looking at the buyers through the glass of a helicopter. It's a picture which captures their air of: "You can't reach us," that is a very important part of the Abba image today. It's an unreal ideal, far away from the everyday life, the society, and the time. In that way, it's a good presentation of the music that Abba have on the record. It's a very effective escape from reality.'

An even more sinister finger of scorn was pointed at them by Roger Wallis, also of *Dagens Nyheters*, who is acknowledged as a spokesman for the 'socialistic' music movement. He said: 'Abba is using blackmail to get orders from record dealers in Sweden,' and went on to claim that the Abba organisation told dealers that they must order at least two or three hundred copies of the 'Arrival' album, or face the prospect of missing out on Christmas deliveries. The retort of the dealers was: 'This is rubbish. We don't have to be blackmailed to stock Abba records. We sell a lot of their records, and we are allowed to buy as few or as many as we want. There is no need to force us into the Abba market. This Abba fever is worse than Beatlemania ever was.'

Abba think a lot of criticism is heaped on them unfairly, and they feel a lot of people look on them as money-grabbers who have no concern about the music they turn out, as long as it is successful. Anni-Frid gets quite angry about it. She said: 'I don't know why it is considered unpleasant to earn money. Everybody does it, I believe. And everybody wants success. Yet when somebody else reaches a pinnacle, they have to put up with a lot of knocking. It is unfair and makes me angry. People forget all the years we had to struggle to get where we are now. Our success wasn't just presented to us on a plate. I know that some people have been comparing us to The Beatles, and using that comparison as a stick to knock us with. That's silly, because The Beatles were a very special phenomenon. We may match them one day, but we'll just have to wait and see.'

A particularly abrasive critic said: 'They are professionals, but aren't they at the same time prey to speculators and commercialism? Aren't they dangerous for the kids who idolise them? It's glittery and it's plastic, a world of dreams and love that isn't true. Is that the message Abba are to spread around the world?'

Bjorn, who has become accustomed to a running battle with this sort of intellectual criticism from the serious-minded Swedish newspapers, retorted: 'We write tunes which please everybody, not just a few critics. If we tried to please the critics, we would get nowhere. Our audiences never criticise us. They buy our records, they know we work hard, and they know they are buying the very best we can make. We don't give a damn about what other people think. We do exactly what we want ourselves, which happens to be what millions of people round the world want. What is so wrong with that? We have never done anything we don't like ourselves. The tunes that become hits carry an image of us. It would be a terrible situation if we were trying to get people to buy stuff we didn't like ourselves.'

His reply to questions about messages and political consciousness was: 'We try to entertain, not to indoctrinate people. We leave the messages to politicians and others who are into that kind of thing. Of course, we discuss politics amongst ourselves and our friends, but where we stand is our own private business.' He was asked if he didn't think everything they did was meaningless. 'Never,' was his reply. 'Not as long as we can make people happy, as we do. Our reward is the audiences who appreciate, the people who write letters to us and tell us the songs are good. We know we have inspired a lot of youngsters to start playing and singing themselves, to start groups and so on. We've made money, yes, but people decide themselves whether they want to buy our records or not. And don't think that we get so much money. Remember, we pay 85 per cent in taxes. The more we earn, the more we give to society. And our main motive is not money.'

Agnetha came in for a bit of double criticism. First, about a solo record, 'Eleven Women in a House', which went out in 1975 and is probably the last solo record she will ever make. Reviewer Mats Olsson said of the song, which is about women's lib: 'Next time, get rid of these ridiculous lines. I want to know Agnetha more than I want to know about a lot of made up people in a house that doesn't exist.' And even her smile came in for some carping. As a youngster, she used to have a gap between her two front teeth. Over the years, this has closed up naturally. But people started to whisper that she'd had an operation on them to close them up and make her more beautiful. She got very angry about this. 'Why do people have to say things like this?' she said. 'I haven't done anything to my teeth since I was eleven years old.'

The Swedish feeling about Abba was epitomised at the time of the 1975 Eurovision Song Contest, which was held in Stockholm only because Abba had won the contest the year before. For when the group requested tickets to go to the contest from Swedish Television, they were refused. A television boss said: 'Any record company with an artiste in the contest is entitled to two tickets. Abba's company has no artistes in the show, so they can't have any tickets. I'm sorry, but we can't make any exceptions.' Abba had to shrug their shoulders and accept that this is the way things are done in Sweden. They had been refused, even though at one time it was planned that Abba should present the trophy to the new winners. That was changed, and one of the elderly television executives made the presentation instead. But they were still upset they could not go, and suspected that the hard-heads of television, who didn't really like them, were behind the decision.

Buyers from foreign television stations are aware of this inbuilt prejudice against Abba. For when they approach Swedish Television to ask for programmes about the group, they are told none are available, and are offered instead programmes on Stockholm, bird life, and other nature films.

'Thank you, but do you have anything on Abba?' ask the exasperated executives. 'That's the only thing we want from Sweden.'

'Well, we have this programme on the Swedish islands . . .'

Swedish Television has studiously avoided Abba, while companies abroad are clamouring for anything on them. They did finally make a film on Abba, but only because Stikkan Andersson pressured them to do the obvious. For the state-controlled Swedish Television reflects the views of the social-democratic Swedish government, to whom pop groups are like a Nordic nightmare, filled with the spectres of decadence and commercialism.

Abba do not seem able to avoid the barbs which are forever

being aimed at them. When they appeared at a pre-wedding gala given at the Stockholm Opera House in the summer of 1976, for King Carl Gustav and his bride to be, Silvia Sommerlath, they included in their repertoire their latest song, 'Dancing Queen', as a tribute to the woman who was to be Sweden's first young Queen in post-war years. It only produced a howl of protest – because they admitted they had not written the song specially for Silvia. Said Benny: 'The song had, in fact, been written a year before and we did plan it as our next single release. But the title was just perfect for the occasion, so we used that song, and I think it was a very nice tribute to our new Queen. Unfortunately, a lot of other people got the wrong idea about it, which was a pity.'

They tried to rescue their prestige in Swedish eyes with the one hour programme for Swedish Television, called 'The Abba Story'. They didn't. For they promised to sing live on the programme, something which the critics said they were scared to do. In the event, two of the numbers appeared live, with seven others as 'sound over' to scenes of them at work and play. Even the two which appeared to be performed live were not all they seemed to be. A technician who worked on the television recording said: 'When I heard the sound on television, it did not tally with what I heard in the studio. The big Abba sound, with multi-track recording, was dubbed on afterwards for television. Their problem is that when they sing live, they sound thin. Not thin compared to four other singers, but compared to the Abba studio sound which we have gotten used to.'

The group's reaction to this is: 'If listeners want the Abba sound they know, we should give it to them. We have learned the techniques of miming to playback tapes, so it's not as if we seem lifeless when we are doing it.'

The national 'knock Abba' pastime even extended to a school in the Stockholm suburbs, which they used for rehearsals. As a 'thank you' to the school for the help, they gave a show in the main hall. The kids loved it, but two of the teachers, who thought the concert was too loud, brought in machines to measure the noise of the concert at 114 decibels. They pointed out that the decibel limit for dance halls was set at 90, and said Abba should have kept to that. The group were flabbergasted by this incredible reaction to their free show for the children. They were too taken aback to express anything but open-mouthed astonishment.

Around the same time, Abba tried to strike a blow on behalf of pop music. The popular 'Top Ten' programme was struck from the schedules of Swedish Radio because the intellectuals and critics said it was not fair on the overall music scene, because people would only buy records that were in the top ten. The four members of Abba wrote an open letter to Stig Ulin, the programme controller who made the decision, protesting that the reason Abba existed as a group was because of the top ten voting every Saturday 'and we think that the programme could provide a boost for Swedish pop music. Don't take the programme away because you will take away some of the Swedish audiences' fun and you will deny Swedish pop music the opportunity of a hearing outside Sweden.' The programme came off, regardless, and their response was a loud silence.

The town where they won the Eurovision Song Contest stepped forward to join the ranks of the Abba knockers when the winning song, 'Waterloo', was 'banned' by the local BBC radio station. Disc jockeys there were angered because Bob Gunnell, the station manager of Radio Brighton, put the song on the restricted list, when it was riding high in the pop charts. Mr Gunnell explained: 'This means that the song will not be played, except for two special programmes of progressive music and a programme for young people. It is my decision and it follows my policy of playing middle of the road music, which has proved successful. This song does not come into that category. Because people are buying it doesn't mean it is the sort of music our listeners want.'

CHAPTER SIXTEEN

# AN ISLAND OF DREAMS

An archipelago of islands, looking like snowflakes scattered on the waves, stretches out from Stockholm, reaching into the deep blue of the Baltic Sea. If you could find a certain tiny island there, and swoop down on it on almost any summer's day, you would find the four youthful and fresh members of Abba and their mastermind, Stikkan Andersson. For this is their island of dreams, where they hide themselves from the turmoil and stress of modern life, where they free their minds to write the songs which have entranced the world. Its location is a closely guarded secret, for if their hideaway was discovered, it would be a hideaway no longer. Even the stern and brooding Swedes produce a younger generation with its share of excitable teenage fans who would descend on the island to strip it of souvenirs and its tranquillity.

The purchase of the tiny island was the idea of Stikkan Andersson, who realised detachment was the ideal help to artistic creation. He says: 'When we are not abroad, we are mostly working, and we work best there on the island. It is our escape, and our salvation.

'It is strange that the more successful we become, the harder we work. Perhaps it is because we know we are expected to do better and better each time. We are always being pushed along by the standards of our last record. So the pressure is always on. The island is one of our answers to that pressure, and I think it is one of the secrets of our success. But as soon as we arrive there, we start working. We can work during the night and sleep during the day if we feel like it. And we don't shave out there, because there's no-one to see us. I think if people did see us out there, we would half scare them to death.'

This is, in fact, their second island of dreams. The first, one called Viggso, just a few miles out from Stockholm, they found themselves driven out of in 1974, because, unfortunately, it was mentioned in the newspapers, and a flood of sightseers followed in the wake of the reports.

'We won't make the same mistake again,' said Stikkan. 'Our new island – just an hour by car and fast boat from the centre of Stockholm – is protected by a wall of silence which I don't think even MI5 could break down. It's a small island, but there is plenty of room for us. We spend as much of springtime and summertime there as we can. But not in the winter. Do you think we're crazy? Do you know how cold it is there in the winter?'

Says Benny: 'When we set off for the island in the boat, it is as if a great door is clanging shut behind me, closing out the rest of the world. I feel the strain of the city draining out of me, and the strains of our music flowing in. Bjorn and I sit around there in the sunshine, searching for the musical phrases. When we have a cluster of pieces of music we feel we can use, we go back to the studios to work on them more systematically. But the island is our inspiration. Away from the telephone calls and the business problems, we can open our uncluttered minds to music.'

For Bjorn, the island is a throwback to the time when, if he felt a problem closing in on him, he would detach himself from the earth by rowing a boat out into the middle of a lake, as he did when Bengt Bernhag died on his wedding day. 'I can only take so much of the hectic tempo of life,' he said. 'When I feel it all building up on me, I know there is only one thing to do. Head for the island. It's strange how putting some water between yourself and the world opens up your mind. When we are rushing around on tour, I dream of our little island. I vividly recall sitting down to an exotic lunch in London once, and all that was on my mind was the island, and the boat. When the pressure builds up on us, and we are all aware when it is happening, we know we must go home and hide for a while. I can't spend too much time there, I know.

'There are many groups who tour the whole year round, and I have no idea how they do it. We couldn't. We could not live from hotel to hotel. That would kill us. And there is no way we could write songs in hotels, as some people do. Our life-style suits us perfectly. We can do what we want to do, and occasionally we will go on tour to show people that we are real, and that we are not just another factory group.'

A factory group Abba certainly are not, and it is their relaxed life-style which means that, while appearing so relaxed and homely, they have had the energy left over to polish their performance until it outshines everyone else around.

Benny laughs when he thinks about his one great luxury on his house on the island. A grand piano. 'I know that sounds incongruous, on the island and back to nature and all that,' he says. 'But I have to have a piano there to work, and why not a grand? Bjorn sits by me, plucking at his guitar, and I can go to town on the keyboard. Sometimes we go days without finding a single bar that we like, but the strange thing is that often we come up with exactly the same ideas about how we want our tunes to work out. It's even stranger when you realise that our tastes in other people's music is so vastly different. I'm still hooked on the classics, like Bach. It could be that my liking for the classics influences my writing. I don't really know. But I think we'll both admit that the paramount influence on us has been The Beatles. Though nowadays, we think of ourselves when we write songs. We have stopped writing songs for other people. If we find a good melody, why should we give it away to someone else? If we think we can sell records with the song, and we like it, we record it ourselves.

'Buying our own island was something we'd promised ourselves for a long time. I don't want that to sound as if we are millionaires, because that is not the case at all. It was not expensive, and cost only about the same as you might pay for a house. What makes it so much better than a house is the miles of deep blue water surrounding it. It gives us the sort of isolation a moated castle used to have, and it's an insulation we take advantage of. It's a great feeling to be in the middle of a hectic and strenuous time, and know the island is always there, waiting to welcome us. And being out of sight means we can relax in our T-shirts and jeans, and be completely ourselves.'

Agnetha does not allow herself to feel left out of it while the boys put their music together. She still writes her own songs, and plans to put them in her own LP. 'Don't take that as a sign I am thinking of leaving Abba,' she said. 'Nothing could be further from the truth. But you don't really expect me to sit around while the boys are at work? I have to do the writing on my own, because that is the only way I can manage it. I can't work with Bjorn in the way he does with Benny. We tried to compose music together once, and we got nowhere and had to agree it could not work out. I don't know why that is. Perhaps it is something in me, or perhaps it is extremely rare that musicians can work together like Benny and Bjorn do.'

Why Abba have been so successful is a question which has intrigued music men since they burst on the world stage. The difference between them and earlier Swedish groups, certainly, can be summed up in one word: professionalism. Before them, music in Sweden was handled in a very amateur way. It was treated like a game rather than a business, with a lot of fooling about and having some fun. Abba, with coaching from Stikkan Andersson, was the first group that put thought behind its carefully and skilfully handled programme. For them, it was no longer a game. It was deadly serious. They put a lot of time in at the studio, and if they got an idea, they would gnaw at it until they had really worked it out. They developed the right way of dressing and presenting themselves onstage. They built up an image of a cool and sophisticated group, which is very much what they are. Suddenly, they were not four young people playing and singing for fun, but four young people writing and singing their own music. Stikkan Andersson's advice and planning made sure they didn't just hammer out records to sell, but worked and worked on their music until they were making records that were one hundred per cent their own product, and which they were one hundred per cent satisfied with. What they produced was a new sound for Sweden, and a new sound for the world. And the two good looking boys combined with the two good looking girls supplied exactly the right ingredients, in exactly the right amounts. It's obvious that they really like each other, and to the listener they spell happiness.

Stikkan Andersson says: 'We have a sophisticated presentation which no other group has even come anywhere near. We have a degree of professionalism which others only dream about. It is something I have taught them from the beginning, and it is something which they have taken over themselves and developed beautifully. We still discuss our performances right down to the very last detail. We run a democracy here, you know. I've always told them to play it cool, and warned them to keep their feet firmly on the ground. It's so easy in this business to get big headed and let success ruin you. This has happened to a lot of people, but there was no way this was going to happen to Abba. For me, it is easy to be the manager, godfather, the fifth member of Abba, because they are intelligent, bright people. They have always been bright enough to take notice of me. I want to make sure that nothing takes us by surprise. We discuss what is happening in different countries, from Israel to Japan, from Hungary to Brazil. They are well informed all the time and, once again, it is teamwork as far as the decisions are concerned. More and more I find I can let them make their own decisions, and they know I would not force them to do anything. I leave it very much up to them. But if I say, "No," to something, they respect my opinion enough never to go ahead and do it. If I say "Yes," they will do it, because they know I have my reasons and their best interests at heart. If it is a major step, I ask them for their feelings about it, and take notice of them. It wasn't always like this. In the early days, I had my plans and they followed them. And they worked out pretty well, didn't they?

'Their life style has not changed very much over the years. Now we are starting to see some money, but in this country you can't take it yourself because if you do you will end up paying eighty-five per-cent in tax. What we can do is build up the company, and this is exactly what I am doing. We intend to get into the art business, which we feel is close to the business we are already in. We buy buildings, shares, bonds, and try to place the money for the future. Don't get the idea we are starving. Far from it. Although on the island, unshaven and wild, it may look that way. We recently moved into new houses in a nice suburb of Stockholm and the girls have bought themselves new sports cars – Agnetha got a BMW, and Anni-Frid a Maserati. But that's about the only change. We still live our lives in very much the same old way. We still work most of the time, and don't have much spare for anything else.'

Bjorn points to the fact that the group came together slowly, evolving over several years instead of being plucked out of the blue. He says: 'Like so many people in show business, we were around for years and years before we became overnight discoveries. We had plenty of time to grow accustomed to what was happening. It didn't creep up on us to take us by surprise. However, we are thankful for the luck we have had, and we know that one day showbusiness will have seen enough of us. But we are ready for that, too.

'The big difference for us these days is that we have to take our work much more seriously than we used to be able to when we were doing things like touring the *folksparks*. In those days, which seem so lighthearted in retrospect, though I'm sure they were not, I don't think any of us had any idea where we were going in the business. I suppose it was more of a hobby then.'

Said Stikkan: 'I know that after English groups like The Beatles were successful, a flood of English groups came on to the market, following them and accepted some reflected glory.

But most of them were not very good. You can't just find talent on any street corner. There were managers who picked a bunch of people, threw them together and, like a creator, said: "This is a group." This happened many times, with managers throwing together kids who looked quite good, and worrying about the music later. And so often they sounded that way. The sound was predictable and often awful, but hidden in the concert halls by the screaming fans.

'The situation with Abba could not have been more unrelated to that sort of approach. They gradually came together to blend into a group by a sort of natural process, rather than a forced gathering of elements. It was a remarkable coincidence, an unbelievable chance, that brought these couples together, let them fall in love, and combined them as a group. Their sound is different, and the concerts aren't full of screaming kids who smother the sound. The audiences listen to them, and appreciate what they hear.

'Theirs is a chemistry which I don't think you could reproduce. And being interested in mathematics and statistics, as I am, I don't think it's even probable that you will find a group with this kind of talent in Sweden, ever again. They have an impact of talent which surfaces only once every ten years in the whole world; perhaps the chances are that the next time such a group comes along, they will emerge in Australia or somewhere like that. That certain intangible chemistry about the group which gets into their performance is the secret, I believe. I think I'll be lucky to see anything like it again.'

The very *difference* of the group, which pop experts thought would go against them in the early days, has been one of their strongest cards. This striking difference has been what so many of their fans have gone for. Musically, they span a gap The Beatles never crossed quite convincingly – they have bridged the generation gap in pop music. When parents hear their children playing Abba records, they're likely to shout out, 'Turn that up,' instead of the more familiar, 'Turn that off.' The sweet harmony of the group also projects itself very strongly. It is also likely that the wholesome – as well as handsome – appearance of the foursome helps. Men find the two girls delightful and girls like Benny and Bjorn. For the adults, it's a pleasure to be able to enjoy watching a group their youngsters like, a group without unpleasant gimmicks like so many other pop stars. With Abba, adults can feel reassured because their kids are watching two nice, clean-cut heterosexual couples. This clean-cut image is the sort which might damage other groups, but it is a large part of Abba's success. The parents as well as the teenagers buy their records. You even find grandmothers going into record stores to buy Abba discs. And parents join their children at the Abba concerts. As one Australian magazine put it: 'Abba are the first to emerge from the dark age of heavy rock and sweep away the cobwebs.'

Said Stikkan Andersson: 'I remember an American promoter coming to a concert we gave here in Stockholm and say he could not believe his eyes when he saw the parents coming with their kids. It astonished him that the age gap could be bridged by the old enemy – pop music.'

Their togetherness is a factor which should not be underestimated in looking for the basis for their success. But even they realise you can have too much of a good thing.

Said Benny: 'I know some people say you should never take your wife to the office, but the close-knit feeling we have is a distinct advantage to Abba. We've had a lot of practice of living and working together, and we know what the others are thinking because of that. This can only help a working relationship. Before we all worked together, we were living together as couples and working separately, and that was much more of a strain.

'I'd say the four of us must like each other a hell of a lot to have spent these past years in each other's pockets and still come out smiling. We are always being asked how we can stand so much of each other, working together, travelling together, taking holidays together. Everybody seems to think it must be a big strain, but it really is not.

'Of course, I'm not talking about a twenty-four-hours-a-day united existence. At one time, we did spend what seemed like every minute of every day together, whether we were working or not. Too much did become a bit oppressive, and we now spend time, quite a bit of time, on our own. We have cut down the time we see each other privately, because we see enough of each other when we are at work. That's sufficient. We know each other well enough that we don't have to put on a mask to cover our feelings; we can be open and honest with each other, an essential if you are to have a relaxed working life, which we need.'

Said Anni-Frid: 'Of course, we get upset and angry with each other from time to time. What bunch of people who spend as much time as we do together would not? The worst thing is on the long tours, like the PR visits to America, and the long flight to Australia. We have to tumble off a tiring flight looking bright and clean and sparkling, even if our bodies are screaming out that it aches and we are valiantly trying to catch up with the time change.'

Anni-Frid puts her own strain on the relationship by often arriving a few minutes late for meetings, and Agnetha, who usually arrives that little bit early, gets angry with her. But these are natural surface problems which do not go deep.

Said Bjorn: 'Our recording sessions can be so hectic that people get the wrong impression about us. Of course, we disagree a lot, especially about the singing, because we have four different ideas to offer about how to do it. But I would like to underline that I think it is just those different ideas thrown into the middle which give us much of what we have together.

'Nowadays, we don't meet Anni-Frid and Benny at parties or social things because we see so much of them professionally. Where Agnetha and I are concerned, we try not to mix business with pleasure. We make it a rule never to talk about music while we're at home. We try to forget about it altogether by ski-ing or boating or having fun with our daughter. If we took our work home to bed, we would end up having nervous breakdowns.'

Stikkan sees the teamwork of the group in a slightly different way. 'They are lucky in that they don't have any ego problems to trip them up,' he said. 'Each one will listen calmly to the ideas of the others, and with an open mind. It's a very healthy group in that respect.

'They are now in the magical state where their records almost sell themselves, and they have come a long, long way in the short time they have been together. They were not a serious partnership till 1973, remember. So it has all happened in the past three or four years.

'But bigger things are waiting for us just around the corner. We have only scratched the United States market as yet, and I'm certain we are going to crack that wide open.

'As that great singer, Al Jolson, said, "Folks, you ain't seen nothing yet." Abba are going to climb to even greater heights, and their music, I know, is going to get better and better. And if I can go out and say no to as many people as possible, without really meaning it, we can draw that careful line which keeps up the demand for us but allows us time to keep up our flow. If I were to let them do all the work they are being offered, they would burn themselves out, and that would be a tragedy for them and for pop music. They have turned on something new, bright, and refreshing which appeals to the world, and I don't want anything to dim their light.'

Abba have soared to stardom by being defiantly different. It is certain that other groups will try to copy them. But the surface trappings will not be enough. To produce the magic of Abba, Bjorn, Benny, Anni-Frid, and Agnetha have unconsciously capitalised on a gift which it is impossible to replace.

The gift is . . .

LOVE.